REFLECTIONS

—of a—

BEACHCOMBER

How to Cope with Disability,
Divorce, and Job Loss

LARRY W. GASSER, PHD

ARCHWAY
PUBLISHING

Archway Publishing books may be ordered
through booksellers or by contacting:

Archway Publishing
1663 Liberty Drive
Bloomington, IN 47403
www.archwaypublishing.com
1-(888)-242-5904

ISBN: 978-1-4808-0546-0 (sc)
ISBN: 978-1-4808-0547-7 (e)

Library of Congress Control Number: 2014932201

Printed in the United States of America

Archway Publishing rev. date: 01/29/2014

Earth's the right place for love:
I don't know where it's likely to go better.

from "Birches," by Robert Frost

Contents

Let Yourself See Your Truth

Chapter 1: Let Yourself See Your Truth 3

Beach Reflection No. 1 7

Haiku No. 1 8

Chapter 2: One Snowy Eve:
What Truth Looks Like When You Are Flat
on Your Back 9

Beach Reflection No. 2 11

Haiku No. 2 12

Chapter 3: The Challenge of Permission 13

Beach Reflection No. 3 14

Haiku No. 3 15

Chapter 4: Yes, I Used the Word "Truth" 16

Beach Reflection No. 4 18

Haiku No. 4 19

Chapter 5: The Mythical Nature of Truth 20

Beach Reflection No. 5 22

Haiku No. 5 23

Chapter 6: The How and Why of Thinking 24

Beach Reflection No. 6 30

Haiku No. 6 31

Chapter 7: All We Think We Know
Remains Conditional upon Further Learning 32

Chapter 8: The Best Choices Are Personal:
I Came to the Beach to Live Close to Sea,
Sand, and Shells 36

Beach Reflection No. 7 37

Diminishment by the Sea

Beach Reflection No. 8 40

Chapter 9: So What That You Are Lame,
Blind, and Sick? 42

Beach Reflection No. 9 44

Haiku No. 7 45

Chapter 10: Denial: God or the Doctor Will Fix Me 46

Beach Reflection No. 10 48

Haiku No. 8 49

Chapter 11: How to Cope with Any Crisis 50

Beach Reflection No. 11 54

Haiku No. 9 55

Chapter 12: How the Four *W*s Act in Practice 56

Chapter 13: The Underpinnings of Human Thought Leading toward Conclusions 65

Beach Reflection No. 12 71

Haiku No. 10 72

Life while Blind

Beach Reflection No. 13 74

Haiku No. 11 75

Chapter 14: Introduction to Life as a Blind Person 76

Haiku No. 12 81

Chapter 15: Workplace Discrimination 82

Beach Reflection No. 14 88

Haiku No. 13 89

Chapter 16: My Wonderful Guide Dog,
Commodore...90

Epitaph.. 102

Beach Reflection No. 15 102

Haiku No. 14 104

Chapter 17: Camping while Blind, or "CWB".. 105

Haiku No. 15 121

Hard Sailing toward a Sense of Purpose

Beach Reflection No. 16 124

Haiku No. 16 124

Chapter 18: Let Each of Us Find the
Purpose of Our Own Unique Lives 125

Beach Reflection No. 17 130

Haiku No. 17 130

Chapter 19: To Face a Sea of Troubles............... 131

Chapter 20: A Comment on Suicide 134

Beach Reflection No. 18 137

Haiku No. 18 138

Chapter 21: Keeping One's Mind in the
Present: What a Bear Does in the Woods.......... 139

Beach Reflection No. 19 147

Haiku No. 19 147

Chapter 22: The Child Is Father of the Man 148

Beach Reflection No. 20.................................. 152

Haiku No. 20.. 154

Chapter 23: Disability as a Moving Target 155

Beach Reflection No. 21 162

Haiku No. 21 163

Chapter 24: Joy in Life despite Diminishing
Returns... 164

Haiku No. 22... 168

Relationships:
The Real Rocket Science

Beach Reflection No. 22 170

Haiku No. 23...171

Chapter 25: The "Truth" and the Self:
How to Go Wrong in Relationships...................172

Beach Reflection No. 23 176

Haiku No. 24... 177

Chapter 26: The Wages of Denial 178

Beach Reflection No. 24 180

Poem No. 1: A Worn-Out Sailor 181

Haiku No. 25.. 183

Chapter 27: Accepting the Right to Choose...... 184

Beach Reflection No. 25.................................. 186

Haiku No. 26.. 186

Chapter 28: Divorce No. 1: Fear of Flying........ 187

Beach Reflection No. 26.................................. 192

Haiku No. 27.. 194

Chapter 29: Three Principles of Living
Relationships.. 195

Beach Reflection No. 27.................................. 200

Haiku No. 28.. 201

Chapter 30: Divorce No. 2: New Marriage,
New Mistakes 202

Beach Reflection No. 28.................................. 207

Haiku No. 29.. 208

Chapter 31: Marriage No. 3: One Way to
Find a Permanent Relationship 209

Poem No. 2: My Proposal to JoAnne 213

Experience Is a Hard School

Beach Reflection No. 29 216

Haiku No. 30.. 220

Chapter 32: To Learn from Experience 221

Beach Reflection No. 30 231

Haiku No. 31 232

Chapter 33: The Pitfalls of Language 233

Haiku No. 32 245

Haiku No. 33 245

Chapter 34: Illustration of Fixed Beliefs 246

Beach Reflection No. 31 252

Haiku No. 34 253

Chapter 35: Judging a Personal Life Track 254

Beach Reflection No. 32 257

Haiku No. 35 258

Chapter 36: A Precious Epiphany 259

Haiku No. 36 261

Chapter 37: Endurance through a Love of Life .. 262

Beach Reflection No. 33 266

Haiku No. 37 267

Introduction

No matter that all my years cycled between hell and high times, I always loved life. My experience of life is that it most closely fits the scientific term "punctuated equilibrium." That is, months of normal or even good or happy times pass quietly and then one is struck by a crisis. The crisis absorbs every emotion, every desire to go back, go away, duck out, or disappear. A saying that we all know is, "Denial is not just a river in Egypt." We all try to solve each crisis we encounter; then the storm passes; we either have weathered it successfully or find ourselves more deeply in a hole. Now none of us wishes to find ourselves in a hole. What we desire is to gain a set of skills that will carry us successfully through our hard times back into good weather. That is why this book is for people who want their lives to work.

This is an optimistic book. That is because I have successfully coped with job losses, divorces, and three disabling conditions. It is also a book of reflections. In my inmost heart I live on the beach. So, "Beach Reflections" and a beach haiku introduce and follow most chapters. All the haiku are my own.

Each success gave me an increase in confidence that I would be able to cope well with the next crisis. However, each crisis exacted a severe price. I don't focus on the dark nights of the soul into which divorce and disability drove me. But those dark nights came and made my struggles acute. Everyone should understand that each critical event begins in depression and denial, possibly progresses through anger and bargaining with God or nature or medical folk, and, with luck, advances into acceptance and forward movement. Many times the process circles back or starts over with each change in health or the appearance of new barriers to happiness. Still, in all these states of mind, finding my way to my own needs and goals brought me back into clarity. In that way I developed strategies of thought worth sharing.

The first of these is my beginning mantra, "Let yourself see your truth." Nothing is more difficult than to allow ourselves to recognize our own needs and, while accommodating the needs of others to the extent possible, carry those needs out in our life choices. Society presents many barriers to self-realization, so we need to be sure of ourselves and believe that our goals for ourselves represent our personal realities.

As a trained scholar, I must acknowledge that this book makes no use of statistical research in the principles of decision making. As far as I know, most self-help books have been written from the viewpoint of personal and professional experience, not from principles based on research. Since my argument is that people benefit most from thinking out issues for themselves, I don't think statistical research to back up my ideas is particularly relevant.

This book is about ways of working out solutions to personal challenges. It is not about the results, or specific opinions; nor is it about specific belief systems.

If we find ourselves and find a path through life that reflects our specific selves, we stand a good chance to lead effective lives. That is my hope and wish for all.

The driving force behind giving ourselves permission to recognize personal needs lies in this basic truth: we all have the right to make whatever personal choices that carry out the vision we have for our own lives.

These thoughts provide the foundation laid out in part 1 of the book.

Parts 2 and 3 explore the errors and realizations that arose from my experience of disability generally and blindness in particular. While these sections reflect a personal perspective, just as many a memoir does, the focus is on the digging out of methods of coping that apply to any disabling condition. They also apply to any personal crisis that comes along to break our hearts or our lives.

Part 4, "Hard Sailing toward a Sense of Purpose," explores a practical philosophy of life. Once we accept responsibility for our own choices, then we are freer to see what we need. Freedom to think leads to the understanding of the truths that define our paths through life. So many philosophies argue that to live in the present is essential that we can take it as axiomatic. What living in the present means, however, is to choose life for ourselves, stick to what we know despite challenges, and grant the right to choose to everyone else. That last is particularly hard for us to do.

The first four parts of the book often mention relationships, but part 5, "Relationships: The Real Rocket Science," details the most important and valuable of my experiences with divorce and remarriage. Here, the focus is back on the right we all possess to choose how we will live. The section also shows what difficulties lie in wait for us when we forget that primary principle. It was the experience of going through two divorces and several girlfriends before I figured out where my errors lay and how to overcome them. That part concludes by describing my eventual success in finding the best life partner anyone could ask for.

Finally, the book concludes by examining how we can learn by experience rather than being dominated by it.

If there is a single, unifying viewpoint in this book, it lies in the following paragraph:

> To be on the trail of the human is to live in the present, believe in the right to choose life, beware of predictable errors of thought, and remember to grant these things to everyone else.
> —LARRY W. GASSER

Acknowledgements

My most personal kudos go to my wife, JoAnne Bouchor, without whose encouragement I may never have broken through my reservations about publishing this book. She also read every draft and understood what I meant to accomplish.

No thanks go far enough to express my gratitude to artist Marjorie Laughlin for her excellent drawings of sea and beach life that enliven the book throughout.

My thanks go out to the many students who enrolled in my final and most creative course offering, "The Existential Self in Fiction and Poetry" at Fort Lewis College in Durango, Colorado from 1991 to 1993. Some of these students read and offered helpful comments on early outlines and drafts.

I also appreciate the key role of Mettje Swift who took over my "Existential Self" class when I needed to enter a blindness skills training program. She also read parts of the early manuscript to offer criticisms that led to my taking up a whole new approach to the subject.

I want to thank Adrianne Pontecorvo and the rest of the staff at Archway Publishing for quick responses while producing this manuscript.

Finally, I owe much to the family and friends with whom I often discussed my book. In particular, my long time friend Mark Coburn kept me inspired by his witty letters and good example of what an author should be doing.

Preface

The beachcomber sat in the sunlight, by a table set with clamshells and sand dollars. Surf swept rhythmically onto the distant shore. The sea air tingled with freshness.

Perhaps, he thought, *it was natural for a person looking back at a long, full life to tell others what he has come to believe.* Now he was more of a beachcomber than a retired professor of English or a former manager of disability services. His last three years of teaching had brought together his goal of stimulating students' personal rapport with literature and writing with his recent 32 hours of coursework in counseling and guidance. He had named the resulting course "The Existential Self in Fiction and Poetry." His merging of classic counseling workshops with reading discussion groups brought home deeper insights from his students than he had ever seen before. In time, it is no surprise that he would begin to think in terms of writing a book. During those same years, he became a fellow with the Colorado Resource Center as a statewide community organizer for people with disabilities. He helped to found two disability related not-for-profit organizations that still operate in Colorado. Besides that, he had spent nearly fifty years passing through one disability after another himself. He concluded his career with five years as a manager of Washington State disability services, first with Services for the Blind and then with the Division of Developmental Disabilities. Did such a background qualify him to explain what he knew?

A car passed, its tires humming. Children's voices echoed down the road a ways, their sharp cries pursuing a small dog's barking.

He would like his immediate family and friends to learn what he knows. He would like to leave them his legacy.

So he says to the children as if to his family, even as the neighborhood children pass beyond hearing, his most important words:

"The truth we can know is about ourselves. Other

truths are not much more than speculation. Like sea turtles, we continue to grow as long as we live."

He considered what else he knew well enough to tell the children, whose voices now faded into the far trees. Surely he had learned how to cope with calamities, since he had faced most of them: multiple disabilities, job loss, divorce, and, well, many lesser troubles.

"Yes," he said to himself at last, "but we have to allow ourselves to see our own truth. It's natural in us to resist what we don't like in ourselves. It takes effort to see truly."

A goldfinch landed on the thistle feeder and chirped to warn others off. The evening sun baked his face. An engine thrums in idle three houses away.

He considered how much children learned through their years of play and social experience. Adults would do well to realize that they, too, continue to learn throughout their lives. Surely he was not the only person who held beliefs that later turned out to be wrong.

He decided to say what he had to say and let others take it as they wished. The man opened his book and began to read his own words.

PART 1

Let Yourself See Your Truth

CHAPTER 1

Let Yourself See Your Truth

HERE IS MY LIFETIME MANTRA: "Let yourself. See. Your truth." No one goes through life chanting, "Let yourself. See. Your Truth." The truths we recognize are forced on us by traumatic experiences, whether divorce, disability, or job loss. I have experienced all three.

I once knew a man whose name was spelled "Jon." I asked him why his name lacked the *h*. He said it was because he'd had the *h* kicked out of him. Well, so have I.

Hard times made me reconsider my way of doing things. During my first professional job loss, my initial feelings were focused on my chairperson's bad behavior. It took a year for me to begin to acknowledge my own mistakes. In particular, I had not related well to women outside of sexual politics. I needed to relate to women through a sense of their humanity, equality, and feelings. After being fired, I put a lot of effort into seeing women's points of view. Previously I had suffered from an excess of masculinity. I did not wish to lose another job because I couldn't relate to women, so I went to work on it.

I speak now to those who react to calamity by wanting to do better. I have little to say to anyone who doesn't face the truth of what led to his hard knocks. It is better to follow the path to lifelong learning.

Job loss, divorce, disabling conditions, and relocating are commonly described as loss and are laid out as processes ranging from denial to acceptance. That notion is fine for some purposes, but the hard knock in question does more: it challenges all our assumptions and ways of dealing with the world. We may not notice that we must change in the face of a calamity. I prefer to see job loss, divorce, and disabling conditions as wake-up calls.

Still, it's hard to decide to cope with trouble when you won't even let yourself see the truth about what's happening. A person can only recognize what he really needs by allowing himself to see who he really is-not only to understand himself but also to live by the real characteristics he discovers through his self-examination.

That's why I focus on the sentence, "Let yourself see your truth." Let's parse the sentence, "Let yourself. See. Your truth." I separated it that way for a reason. Really, the first two words-the subject-speak to giving yourself permission. One of the hardest challenges I ever faced was to let myself see that my first wife was beginning a love affair. I saw the signs. I felt the fear. At one cocktail party, the man followed her around as if he were her puppy. After everyone left, I complained. She just said, "I'll take care of it." I let her get away with that dismissal. A person is likely to respond submissively when he doesn't let himself see his truth.

For most of us, it takes disaster to make us let ourselves see the truth of our lives and our circumstances. It's too bad it takes such force to make us acknowledge truths we haven't previously allowed ourselves to see. During the time I did disability work, I saw that many disabled people did their best to hide vision loss, epilepsy, MS, or mental illness. Those with dyslexia avoided writing. Those with bipolar disorder often refused medication.

I met addicts who believed their drug or alcohol usage was perfectly normal. One man I know, while working off a DUI, kept driving and even had his friends sign to verify he had gone to his required AA meetings. Sometimes it takes a lot of work to hide from yourself.

I finally did have to face the truth that my first wife was having an affair. It was just so difficult to face what I knew would be a very hard thing to get through. I didn't want to go through it, so I didn't let myself see it for a long time.

First, like most people, I needed to give myself permission, but the middle part of my mantra sentence, the verb *see*, poses another set of challenges. To see something, we must have an inclination to watch life, do self-examination when called for, and maybe even begin to believe our intuitions. To see also implies a willingness to act on what we see. Once you see your wife is having an affair, that your vision loss is interfering with your daily life, or that your arthritic joints have caused you to drop out of sports, then you take actions to deal with the situation. Finally, the object of the sentence, "the truth," says you have let yourself see what is really going on. You realize that if you don't act on what you know, things will get worse. For example, once I hired a person

I knew in my heart was a bad choice. Yet she had performed best during the interview. Soon everyone in her program wanted to quit. I overrode the truth I saw based on a misplaced ideal. I revised my ideas about hiring.

Let yourself see the truth, and act on it. Things work out better that way.

BEACH REFLECTION NO. 1

On South Beach, by Westport, Washington, dark sand stretches away out of sight both north and south. Many sand dollars, occasional clamshells, and infrequent agates lie about. Few days go by when the beachcomber does not wander up and down the damp sand. He lets his guide dog, Commodore, run along all the logs washed up near the dune as he pulls out the flexi-lead to its full extension.

As he walks, watches his dog, and spots other combers, he meditates on all the living that had caught him in its toils. Yet the feel of the sand grinding under his feet, the salt smell of the sea, the washed-up kelp, and birds in the sky all catch his attention. If any of it had meaning, then all of it had meaning.

But what does a beach mean? He considered that people make of it what they will, but that does not alter its reality. The answer is that it means what it is. So, he concluded, there is self, with all its memories, and there is reality, its odors and wash of sounds. Keeping the two straight had to be important.

HAIKU NO. 1

On a chilly beach
among sand dollars and stones
a seagull dances.

CHAPTER 2

One Snowy Eve:
What Truth Looks Like When
You Are Flat on Your Back

ONE SNOWY EVE, I WALKED past Mr. Rosewater's Deli in Durango, Colorado, onto an icy and uncleared sidewalk fronting a parking lot. I walked carefully on my slick shoes. In the next moment, I lay flat on my back, staring up into light snow flurries dropping from the black sky.

Well, I thought, *I must have fallen.* Funny, I didn't hurt anywhere. No muscle was strained, the back of my head lay comfortably on the icy sidewalk, and my hands were at my sides. Truly, I simply had no memory of any transition from walking to lying supine under snowflakes. Surely I would have injured myself by falling so suddenly that I couldn't even try to catch myself with feet or hands. Normally we get hurt when we fall. No, I lay comfortable and warm on the ice in my London Fog overcoat and stocking cap. Snowflakes falling on my face glittered quite beautifully.

I began the process of making up an explanation for how I came to be lying full length on an icy city sidewalk. Perhaps the surface was so completely without friction that my feet had shot forward and my body remained so relaxed because I had no perception of the situation. I had luckily come down smoothly and comfortably.

However, the truth is, I have no idea how I got there. No explanation seemed to be convincing. The fact that I was unhurt just made it all impossible to account for. Probably there are people who would call it an act of God. Others may argue that I just didn't remember slipping. Perhaps acrobatic types may observe that I must have slapped the sidewalk to break my fall the way they and other athletes do.

Such happenings do not arrive with explanations. They are inarticulate moments, as are all sudden events. I could not connect the event of my transition from walking to lying on the icy sidewalk. There were no witnesses-no one around to tell me what they saw. Even if there were, we all know how unreliable witnesses can be. It was real but beyond explanation. My attempt to explain most probably had no connection with the event. First came the event and then my human attempt to explain. That is, in fact, how life happens to us. Events, actions, surprises, and existence itself hit us first, and then we try to put them into a human perspective.

Since no conclusion offered itself, I gave up on explanations. But a way to walk more safely on either icy or snow-covered sidewalks occurred to me, and I walked back into town to buy some snow boots.

BEACH REFLECTION NO. 2

One January night a storm passed through our coastal community. In the morning, the beachcomber walked the path down to the shore. As he approached the first dune, he began to encounter first sticks and then larger logs. He soon realized the tide had come over the dune and run down the path. A sense of threat rose in him. Soon he stood on the peak of the dune and watched as a foaming tide swelled to the top edge of the dune and foamed there like boiling water.

Did the ocean mean to scare him? No, that came from his purely human response to the natural action of storm and tide. He sat on a log and tried to relax. Twice more a rising tide foamed at the dune's ridge.

Thinking it could wash over and him with it, he walked back up the path to his home. He would return another day.

HAIKU NO. 2

Cranberries grow wild
tiny sprigs along the path.
Beachcombers pick them.

CHAPTER 3

The Challenge of Permission

IT'S NOT TOO MUCH TO say that all of us are raised to control our behavior with strong inhibitions. Patterns such as modesty, courtesy, and morality, contain sets of inhibitions restricting what we can do or say in social situations. No doubt many inhibitions make sense, but many others do not. A simple example is how my blind friend's teenaged daughter entreated us to be embarrassed about our use of blind canes. Her adolescent fear of standing out in any way made her project her embarrassment on us. Adults abandon such useless inhibitions in order to function fully in life.

We come closer to finding our true selves when

we examine learned inhibitions and drop those that cloud our true selves. Whenever we repress our true responses to events, situations, and people, we only obscure what is true in ourselves. It is more damaging to lie to ourselves than to lie to others. Yet we humans often do lie to ourselves. If we do that, how likely is it that we will ever recognize the truth of our own lives?

That's why I say that my title sentence is the whole problem and the whole solution for dealing with our personal crises. I mean, of course, the three parts of the sentence, Let yourself see your truth. Taken together, they tell the subject, predicate, and object of what I had to learn to make my life work.

BEACH REFLECTION NO. 3

A small home in a small community gains by sitting 1,500 feet from the Pacific Ocean. Set back from a small road and dressed by groves of pines on three sides, the little home reverberates night and day to the distant roar of surf. Just behind rises what many years ago was the first dune. Then, this was the shore. In harmony with this environment, he asks guests to return from their walks to the beach with white quartz stones. He asks them to make wishes and lay the stones on his path.

The sea is the sea, the beach is the beach, but he can manufacture a way of life from this beloved environment. That closes the gap between self and sea.

HAIKU NO. 3

Brown pelicans drop
skydivers intent on prey.
Waves roll onto shore.

CHAPTER 4

Yes, I Used the Word "Truth"

"TRUTH" PROBABLY HAS MORE MEANINGS than trees have leaves. We have religious truth, courtroom truth ("I swear to tell the truth..."), true believer kinds of truth, and scientific truth, to mention but a few. The best path through this tangle of underbrush is to name the very tiny area of truth that I am talking about.

Many who read this book probably will have a habit of thinking things out for themselves. They are on the right track, though the track goes beyond that. This book may also encourage others to begin to think for themselves.

Sometimes circumstances intimidate people to

the point where they cannot embrace life on their own terms. Those who have walled themselves inside a doctrinaire system of belief probably cannot dare to think outside the doctrine. I cannot and will not join them inside their boxes.

Aspects of this book will likely anger many people. I am one of those who believe that anger lets us know where we most doubt ourselves. Perhaps their doctrine does not have as strong a hold on them as they think it does.

First, let's offer the negatives. When it comes to managing our lives, no universal truth exists. There is no truth for people who must believe others are wrong before they can feel they are right. Any group that believes only they know "the truth" are categorically wrong. On the contrary, respect for other people's opinions enhances our humanity. There is no truth in the argument that God has given us all the same mission in life. Rather, many writers think we have specific and concrete missions inside ourselves. I also subscribe to our right to guide our own lives. An individual may choose a religious or spiritual mission for his own life, of course. Each of us is responsible for choosing goals that fit us personally. At the same time, we possess the right to discuss each other's beliefs.

Neither do I accept the idea of situational truths, sometimes called moral relativity. Not only are we individuals; we are part of our communities and everything else that exists. Our challenge is to balance personal with public needs.

Here is what I mean by "truth." Instead of general truths, we are gifted with specific truths that fit our own lives. Truth is about what makes us function successfully in this complex world. Because we come into life trailing clouds of billions of chromosomal potentials, each of us combines some degree of difference from everyone else. To that degree, the way we manage our lives needs to reflect our particular combination of traits.

In this book, then, truth means making decisions that bring our personal traits into the fullest fruition they can reach. Thus, I define truth for this book in personal and individual terms.

There are other kinds of truth. I do not speak for or to those sorts of truths.

BEACH REFLECTION NO. 4

On a given day there might be one other person walking the beach. It's the best time to settle in a chair to let the endless work of tide wash its sounds over you, drenching you in its work of breaking down rocks into sand. A crow flies by croaking raucously; the minor shape of a fishing boat passes far out to sea. A steady wind presses from the south. Several waves out, a seal lifts its head for a moment. You are there with it all, doing your best not to think about anything. Being on shore facing oncoming waves is enough.

HAIKU NO. 4

The sea's endless fall
fills the air, rumbles the ground,
yet shores hold the sea.

CHAPTER 5

The Mythical Nature of Truth

WHAT DOES IT TAKE TO discover any one truth that fits any situation? We don't see as well as eagles, hear or smell as well as dogs, or feel as sensitively as mouse or cat whiskers. Perhaps our taste buds come closest to competing with the ability to taste possessed by other animals; I don't know. The point is that our physical perceptions are pretty limited. We humans can't even agree about the most simple events that happen to us. Even worse, our own minds often don't let us see past our own stubborn misconceptions. Yet we still speak of infinity.

My first wife once said to me that we could stay married if I would accept her lover. She does not remember saying that. Who is right? We don't know for sure, do we? We feel sure, but it doesn't take a lot of experience to realize how often we are in error about the belief of which we felt most sure.

While I was a student, myself, one of my professors told me that being sure was an emotion like any other. As a feeling, it may be accurate or not. It may fit the moment or not. You can feel sure when you are grossly wrong. In short, he meant to remind me of what all scholars need to remember: conclusions need to be left open to revision as our knowledge improves.

By this time of my life, I'm painfully aware of how many times my conclusions or understandings have been rudely corrected.

So what I mean by seeing the truth is seeing clearly how things stand for us, personally. I mean that we need to listen to our intuitions and bodily responses about how we really feel about events. We need to understand how our personal experience of things relates to who we really are. We can't define ourselves by who others think we are, or what we might suppose we should be.

At the same time, we can learn a lot from other people.

For example, good counselors approach their work

by understanding that clients contain the answers to their own dilemmas. The counselor's job is to help them find their own solutions.

First, to make effective decisions, we need to let ourselves see things as they are and especially how they affect us and our own lives. The biggest barrier to doing that, for me, is to let myself do that. Part of my story lays out the anatomy of stubbornness. I'm not alone in refusing to recognize whatever doesn't fit the way I want things to be.

Once I rode one of the twisting canyon roads up from Salt Lake City with a Mormon geologist and friend. As we wound uphill, we passed large signs proclaiming age after age of each geological stratum. I asked him how he could be a Mormon who believed the earth was some six thousand years old as we passed multiple millions of years of earth's rocky evolution. "Oh," he said, "you just compartmentalize religion and science into separate parts of your mind." As for myself, I've found life difficult to live even while keeping my mind and my beliefs in one whole understanding.

BEACH REFLECTION NO. 5

Once the beachcomber found a silver minnow flopping in the ebbing tide. The sea, wind, and shore did nothing to help, so he bent, wetted hands, raised the silver minnow, and walked it deeper into the surf. He dropped it into the water flushing about his ankles.

Did his action make a difference? He remembered Albert Einstein saying that "God does not play dice with the universe." Wet shoes to the contrary, what matters is that he decided.

HAIKU NO. 5

A murder of crows
croaks out a raucous conclave.
Now the sea whispers.

CHAPTER 6

The How and Why of Thinking

HOW TO THINK IS AS important as what to think about. We humans have a unique freedom to make our lives what we want them to be. To live by our own needs while remaining aware of life in the present tense makes sorting out an effective line of conduct way easier than trying to meet what a lot of other people want you to do.

We all have read novels involving a young person in the process of growing up. We share their confusions, celebrate their epiphanies, and applaud their progress. One of my personal growing-up stories is not my favorite one, because my own failures hurt me and others as I made life-damaging errors.

While in my first year of college, I continued to drive a wheat truck during harvest. One hot day, the work crew of men stood by the combine to discuss a repair. The broad pan that enclosed the fan that in turn blew the chaff away from the grain had cracked from the center to the edge. I was the truck driver, whose job it was to load the bed of the truck with wheat while the combine moved through the field. I knew nothing about repairs to any mechanisms. Mr. Book Reader, was I. So I stood apart and watched the men and breathed in the dusty air of the wheat field.

A hazy dome of sky held all the heat any harvest time could boast. The dirt lay hot under my boots. Had I stayed seated in the truck, I would have been asleep by now. That wouldn't do. Darrell, the farmer, had awakened me once already this week. My trick of lightly bracing a foot against the open truck door so that if I relaxed my foot would drop and waken me. My foot had not dropped, but my heart did when Darrell rapped on the truck door.

"Ready to go to work?" he said. Then he walked back to the combine before I could answer.

In me lay the impulse to be part of the operation, but I just didn't see how. I stepped closer to the men to hear what they said and to seem more involved.

"The pan is tin. We'll have to braise it," Darrell said.

"I'd rather weld. Don't have too much chance to braise things." The speaker was a man whose eyes never stopped moving. Well, maybe he paused a click to connect with Darrell, but otherwise kept his eyes bouncing over the rounded slopes of the field.

"Can't weld tin. Got to braise," Darrell said. "Have you got the stuff?"

The men broke from their cluster, each to go for the right tool or whatever else they felt was needed. It made me even more self-conscious. They seemed to know what to do even without speech. They knew how to bustle, when I only knew how to watch. Yet the one man seemed to have watched everything around and about without pause while decisions were made. Maybe, I thought, I don't even know how to watch. Can you watch when you don't even know what's going on? I still felt the dirt heating my boots. I remembered the weasel I had flushed from the wheat during their last breakdown. It had tried to run. I had caught it with my boot and held it down while it chewed along the sole. Then it stiffened. I lifted my boot to look more closely, and it leapt to its feet and ran into the ditch. I couldn't find it again. What a perfect example of watching but not knowing, not understanding.

The man with the jumpy eyes came around with his equipment and soon began braising the tear in the pan. He had liberal advice from the rest of the crew as the bead drew itself across the tin of the broad pan. I decided I could use the time to grease all the zirks on the truck. I made sure the grease gun was loaded and got busy. Working slowly to stretch the task, by the time I looked back at the crew, one of them was reorganizing tools atop the combine, and jumpy eyes dug in the dome of wheat that had poured underneath the combine when the pan had been removed. Apparently a tool was missing.

Suddenly I noticed the man atop the combine kick off a huge wrench used on the massive bolts that held the sides of the combine. Jumpy eyes below quickly leaped back without looking up. The massive wrench dropped exactly into the center of the wheat dome. Grain sprayed aside from the heavy impact.

"Sorry," the man atop the combine said.

I just stared. I breathed again in awe. How had jumpy eyes seen the wrench falling when he had not been looking? How did he know? I had not heard any noise when the wrench was kicked off the combine. It made no noise falling. I just felt awestruck.

"No problem," jumpy eyes said.

In the bunkhouse that evening, I learned that

jumpy eyes had been on the Bataan death march. Maybe he survived because he watched everything all the time. Now I felt sure that while I, myself, watched, I had not really seen anything. Perhaps really to see was to see with understanding, seeing so merged with an intuitive grasp of things that no time separated sensing and responding.

I felt even more ignorant the next day when Darrell asked why I had not helped with the repair. I answered that I didn't know anything about it.

Darrell said, "You could have asked or even helped clean up. You can see that things needed cleaning up, couldn't you?" Now I wondered how there could be so much missing in me. I was enrolled in college. I had read many books. I felt I meant well and wished to be liked, perhaps even valued. Yet this new situation made me experience the same sense of being a stranger in a strange land that I had felt in every new town.

The next evening when I and the farmer's daughter, Linda, hit the road for Grand Coulee Dam, I drove my father's Pontiac swiftly and casually along the narrow, two-lane road that led to the dam. She asked me to slow down, but that just irritated me. In my heart, though, I knew the old road, with its rising and falling, its old patches and country turns wasn't a good road to speed on. Later, I let the speed decline after it couldn't be connected to her request.

These are the kinds of situations when a person most needs self-knowledge. Even more, a person needs to embrace that self-knowledge and decide behavior accordingly. Even if my driving was excellent, as I thought, it would have been nice, even courteous, to slow up even if just to please my passenger.

Later, with the dam's spillway lit by coruscating and color-shifting lamps, I sang "With the Wind and the Rain in Her Hair" to her. Here was something I did seem to know: girls liked you to sing to them. At least I knew something. What I didn't know, and what led to another life-changing mistake, was that I was creating a depth of feelings in Linda that I could not match, later. In those days it seemed natural to pour out all the charm I possessed. In that fall, it became clear to me that Linda wanted to marry me and, indeed, that had been her parents' intention as well. I panicked, and in my panic, I stopped writing to her. Oh, so many times I have wished to apologize first for engaging her love more than I could reward, and second for cutting off communication. Perhaps the worst act is to freeze when you don't know what you are doing. That is the consequence of giving way to fear. Any action is better than silence by the ethics I have evolved for myself since then.

Not writing did not end the consequences. The next summer, I returned to what I thought was my annual summer job driving a wheat truck for Darrell. He had fired me. I then walked over to the grain elevator, where I had worked for two summers, and found that, there, too, I had been fired. Here was a double lesson, one being my own fault, and the other deriving its power from the small town. The elevator operator's wife was a close friend of Linda's mother. Sometimes the overripe apple rolls far from the tree.

BEACH REFLECTION NO. 6

His daughter discovered a crude oil-soaked seagull on the beach. Not only could it not fly, it could barely walk. A passerby told her to let it alone because it would die, anyway. She couldn't agree. She couldn't just leave it, struggling and flopping about so miserably.

She hurried back to the house, got a box, came back to the beach, and scooped the bird into it. She called around to find an animal rescue organization and delivered the oil-soaked gull there on her way to the airport.

We don't know if the gull lived or died, but it was her decision to make. And she did it despite discouragement from the passerby.

HAIKU NO. 6

A crude oil-soaked gull
flops like a large stranded fish
on a barren beach.

CHAPTER 7

All We Think We Know Remains Conditional upon Further Learning

I TAKE IT AS COMMON knowledge that babies are born with a certain temperament and general traits. Some tend toward a high activity level, some to a lower activity level. Some develop faster than others in relation to child developmental stages. As to knowledge, babies can't talk or operate their limbs in an organized manner. All that human society can do and all human knowledge remains to be learned.

I also take it as common knowledge that we continue to learn about our world all the way through our life span.

As we grow, our personally inherited qualities

influence how we react to our environments. Our traits also direct how and what we learn. Our unique consciousness filters the influences that surround us and the experiences we encounter. Somewhere along the line we begin to interpret experience and draw conclusions. Our conclusions constitute the things we think we know.

Granted that our conclusions arise from our selfhood, our personal experiences, and the cultural environment that surrounds us. Even so, we are called upon to examine our beliefs to see which of them stand up to our actual encounters. To accept ideas blindly is to live blindly, and I am speaking of metaphorical blindness. It isn't a question of eyesight, but of insight.

Just because things happen doesn't mean we understand those things. I offer my sidewalk experience as a template of how our minds work to understand the inarticulate reality into which we are born. It is as natural as breathing to try to understand events. What we need to remember is that understanding is an act of interpretation, not truth itself.

Some of us are able to leave questions open, at least until we get more experience or information. Some quality we possess allows us to recognize our limitations. The best contrast to openness I know of lies in the continuous efforts people make to explain who shot and killed former President John F. Kennedy. Others of that ilk give a fanatic belief to a particular conspiracy theory. I don't claim to understand why humans are so able to argue passionately for a conclusion so patently beyond convincing evidence. There you have the opposite poles of how we humans react to what we think we know. Some of us can leave our conclusions tentative pending further experience or information; others of us must cling to a sense of security drawn from having their minds made up.

So many of my past certainties have been upset by new knowledge that I hesitate to form anything more than working hypotheses. One must make decisions without complete information all through life. I am comfortable with that as long as I've listened to myself and done the best I can to think through each issue.

I remember a dinnertime conversation I had with one of my professors while I was working on my master's degree. He mentioned how poorly the Lummi Island Indians were being treated. I don't remember my exact words, but I asked something about what can be done for drunken Indians. My professor asked me how I could misunderstand their lives so badly. I simply could not defend expressing an opinion based neither upon thought nor information. Naturally, it embarrassed me to have made a foolish observation. Unlike me, some individuals would cling to their opinion just because another person challenged them. In my case, it was simple and ignorant prejudice. Only after eighteen years among Navaho, Southern Ute, Jicarilla Apache, and Pueblo Indians did I begin to have some informed understanding about the lives of Native Americans. Even so, I would still rather ask them for information than state a conclusion about their lives.

Start by understanding that human beings have created what we think we know. Our task in growing up is to evaluate what knowledge we've picked up from others. Then, to be mature obligates us to pick and choose the conclusions by which we intend to live.

CHAPTER 8

The Best Choices Are Personal: I Came to the Beach to Live Close to Sea, Sand, and Shells

I CAME TO WESTPORT TO live the life of a beachcomber. A window open at night allows the deep and distant roar into the bedroom where it lulls me into sleep. To step onto my deck is to step into the purest air in America. As I walk to the beach, I am surrounded by all the birds, deer, raccoon, and sometimes even bears. All is natural and sane.

I got to this peaceful place by letting myself understand the meaning of events as they applied to me. It is not so easy to give yourself permission to live by your own way of looking at things rather than how others might argue. But I never could succeed in living by someone else's understanding.

Even if I have "let myself" think for myself, the next challenge is to "see." Now, my vision is barely adequate to discerning a bright window. So when I use the word "see," I mean to recognize what is actually there. When I slipped and fell that snowy eve, I did not attempt to believe I understood the situation. When I lost my job, it took time for me to put aside my defenses to "see" what actually occurred. It may take time to see through your habitual defenses and stubborn misconceptions, but it is the path to personal revelations.

My word "truth" presents a definite challenge. What is true for me may not be so for others. What is important is not what is true for each of us, but how we arrive at what is real and true for each of us, ourselves. We decide personal truths for ourselves because those are the truths we live by.

BEACH REFLECTION NO. 7

Think of "truth" as beachcombers would: some dress in cotton warm-ups, some in wool, and some in nylon windbreakers. One woman wore a dress, for goodness sakes! Each of them made a personal choice.

Only a clothing fanatic would wish a uniform dress code for beachwear. No more should we for personal values.

This beachcomber dressed in rubber-coated rainwear, coat and pants, with rubber boots. When he squatted on sea-washed sand to gather stones, he did not care who wondered at his actions. It could not matter less to him that he never saw any other adult sit down on the wet sand. And he did not care whether others wore bikinis, jeans, or camouflage as long as they neither talked nor threw out trash.

PART 2

Diminishment by the Sea

BEACH REFLECTION NO. 8

He felt like an old sailor as he sat on the shore in his canvas chair. Wasn't he, indeed, under the entrancement of now and then? Both? He knows he should live in the present, celebrate the smell of sea, the rush of sea life about him, and the glitter of stones in the darkness of sand.

However, he needed to think what was left to him now that he was both lame and blind. Not many people would understand what he loved about the beach he could neither see well nor walk upon.

As he sat, surf continued its eternal and rhythmic swamping of the sand. Seagulls screeched in the sky above his head. A little farther down the beach, he heard a Vietnamese family-he guessed-working a fishing pole and cleaning and cooking sea perch over a small fire.

He knew some would wonder how he knew these things, blind and lame as he was. Well, he still had his brain, didn't he? It lay stored with seventy years of experiences, most of them while he could see. Then, too, he could smell and hear things just fine, not better because he was blind, bugger to those who like that explanation, but because now he needed to use those senses.

The greatness of the ocean calmed him. As a

sailor, he had floated on the huge breast of the largest body of water in the world. It swelled with grandeur and immense power. He felt it still, even sitting by its side here onshore.

In such a place as this, he felt it to be time to tell about disability. He could also speak of divorce and job loss, but he knew more people would fear the impact on themselves of disability. Oh, you did cope with these calamities using similar methods, but disability seemed to take more away than the others.

Suddenly a wave rushed at him and laved his shoes in saltwater, chill and rushing. As it ebbed, he picked up his chair and backed up the beach. Damn his inattention to the seventh wave. It caught him again and again. That would teach him to woolgather in the face of a living sea.

CHAPTER 9

So What That You Are Lame, Blind, and Sick?

Life is a process of growing, emerging and reaching out.
—PETER KOSTENBAUM

MY FIRST DISABLING CONDITION HIT me when I was twenty-five years old. Since then, I have had a lifelong slide into deeper and deeper disability. It began with a frozen right ankle, a mysterious arthritis, to escalating joint damage, to Crohn's disease and intestinal bleeding, to eye inflammation with progressive blindness from glaucoma, to kidney failure and subsequent peritoneal dialysis. All of this took forty-five years to develop.

Not even divorce or job loss tested me to the

depths of my soul. No other experiences brought me to the edge of death. No other set of events showed me why life was so precious. Without my long plunge into disability, I would never have personally experienced social and workplace discrimination or been forced to change all my habits of life. I had many moments when I wondered how I could survive each loss of capacity.

For the moment, put aside the medical implications of arthritis, Crohn's disease, or glaucoma. The important issue arises from losses that come about through these conditions. Arthritis eventually ended any athleticism I tried, from basketball to skiing. Crohn's disease gave me pain, internal bleeding, and anemia before hospitalizing me in 1980. The disease itself and my absorption in it contributed to my two divorces.

Then, there was the blindness. What could have been worse? It gradually made me a man who could no longer drive a car, an English professor who could not read print or even his own notes; and a husband who could not see his wife's significant glances.

With any of these conditions, it might seem natural for life to just stop cold. Nothing would b less true. During the time I had to walk with a cane to support my painfully arthritic leg, I spent a year teaching in England. That year, I spent time in the Netherlands, Spain, Italy, and Greece. Rigid ski boots allowed me to use skiing to replace basketball. When I could no longer ski, I took up barbershop singing and a career of fifteen local theater productions during a six-year period. I did all this while teaching full time and losing my eyesight. Now, weak from years of diminishment and deep weakness from kidney failure, what I have left is reading e-texts and enjoying family and friends.

What you and I need to know is that life goes on. But just how does it go on?

BEACH REFLECTION NO. 9

Only a wayward path across the salt grass or a long walk up the beach brought you to a place of logs. Some lie about; others stick up from the sand like ancient pediments. They are the past erosion of the land and even forgotten history. Here is the best place to think that South Beach offers.

Wind soughs past the spars and over salt grass. A crow lands nearby and releases a raucous call. Then he is off, flapping heavily at air until wind lifts him away.

The beachcomber spots a twisted piece of driftwood a few feet away. He looks it over.

"Why," he thinks, "it would dress nicely beside

a beautifully straight-stemmed Dahlia grown by a friend. She could enter into the local flower competition. He felt a deep satisfaction. There was much to be said for a beach.

HAIKU NO. 7

He watches the waves
counting to find a pattern,
surf like sparkling wine.

CHAPTER 10

Denial: God or the Doctor Will Fix Me

IT IS HARD TO IMAGINE anyone being prepared to be disabled. For most people, blindness or crippling or heart disease drops from the sky like a sudden thundershower. It may even come from the shock of an automobile accident or a fall in a spot where we walk every day.

Some of us are born with a disability, but the rest of us wake to it in surprise accompanied by a sense of desperate denial. It just can't be happening.

How true it is that young people have no sense either of disease, disability, or mortality. It isn't that life comes easy to a child. My childhood and young adult peers offered me as many offenses as any adult experiences. My broken leg at five years old, bicycle crashes, fights, and embarrassments gave me true twinges of pain, yes, but years passed before consequences were permanent. My high school years featured more successes than failures as I became the lead scorer in basketball, starting pitcher in baseball, the lead in plays, first clarinet in orchestra, and so forth. I was even selected for the 1959 All Northwest Concert Band. I like to joke that I graduated third in my class ... out of five graduates.

No one my age would have noticed the dire warning implicit in the weeklong series of muscle spasms that kept me out of playing basketball. Doctors would later tell me that those spasms were an early warning of Crohn's disease.

I went off to college and later service in the Naval Reserve with the complete confidence in the future that comes so easily to young people. College was good to me. I played clarinet in the orchestra, sang in the college choir, and played basketball with my brother's AAU club. I slipped in two years of active duty in the Naval Reserve and went back to school rather more serious about life than when I left.

I got married in 1964 to an attractive woman, finished one degree, and began another in 1965. My life had been good. That year was the end of the youthful honeymoon. No matter whether a person has had a lot of success or a more or less hard life, the onset of disability changes everything: work, marriage, and everyday occupations.

We all know the saying that "All good things must come to an end." Sure, many people apparently get through life without a disability, but the rest of us could benefit from opening our minds to what might happen sometime, and most unexpectedly. Many of my disabled friends refer to those without a disability as "TABs," or "temporarily able-bodied." Consider the implications of that term. I know a couple who returned from their honeymoon to a diagnosis of breast cancer for the new wife.

One of my purposes is to explain how to come through hard times and yet to retain confidence in one's self and love of life. Disability is no respecter of age, social status, personal health, or the best of a healthful set of life choices. Readiness to face a crisis is relevant to all of us.

BEACH REFLECTION NO. 10

In time, the man could no longer either walk far or without a walker. Now his beach access came by clinging to his wife or brother as he braved the soft sands leading down to the edge of the recent high tide. Later, he even lost that. Finally, it took a four-wheel-drive vehicle to get him there. Beach visits came to be rare. This meant he was no longer alone. To him, the shore swarmed with company.

As he scanned near his chair for the white quartz stones that used to concentrate his attention, now he watched grandchildren raise castles in sand, or wade through the light wash of retreating tide. Not even the cold wash of the Washington sea could discourage the children. Yet here he was, bundled warmly against the wind. Surely his experience of the beach held no point of comparison with that of the children. Their mother only waded with them out of care for their safety. He couldn't even do that if he wanted to. And he didn't want to.

He realized that each person saw the beach, and therefore life, differently. He just couldn't understand why most people didn't seem to realize how much they differed from one another.

HAIKU NO. 8

My trees are barren
and a chill wind blows no good
through their trembling limbs.

CHAPTER 11

How to Cope with Any Crisis

FOUR CATEGORIES MAKE IT POSSIBLE to cope successfully with personal calamities.

Experts in various fields have come up with memorable acronyms such as KISS for "Keep it simple, stupid," or the three words, "the will, the well, and the wisdom." The first refers to an approach to speaking and writing, whereas the last points at three areas by which to guide decision making. I am going to use these three *w*'s to anchor three of the four ways to cope with disability. However, I will add another *w* for the word "way." Then we have the four: the will, the well, the way, and the wisdom.

1. THE WILL.

Whether you call it determination, desire to strive, or persistence, these qualities are of first importance if you want to cope with life's crises. Perhaps I was lucky to be born stubborn. That is a form of will. After all, it is a family trait. What sort of sport could I have played after having an ankle freeze up on me? Or how could I have continued to teach reading and writing after I could no longer see print? It wasn't easy, but being stopped in one way just provoked my stubbornness not to quit. One of my friends, Jerry Kuns, told me that after he had both eyes removed, a friend of his said, "Don't fade out on us, Jerry." In a time when we deny the problem facing us, we might be very prone to fading out. That is giving up. Can we give up, or do we have the will to overcome the apparent disaster? Do we have the will to push through the barriers we face?

2. THE WELL.

Water wells are named for holes dug deep that allow water to "well" up in them so we can have all the water we need. Call it a water resource. The well, then, is a good metaphor for the resources a person needs to face disability. After all, what do any of us know about being lame, going blind, or dealing with seizures or multiple sclerosis, or cancer? Somewhere there is the help we need. We can reach out to both individuals and organizations that have long experience with our conditions. They will have pioneered most of the attitudes and adaptations we will need. When I began going blind, I joined the National Federation of the Blind. Members of local chapters explained the federation's philosophy of blindness-that it was a nuisance--not a disaster--and that many methods existed to support a set of normal life activities. Most useful was the moral support they offered. The first thing you lose with a disability is your confidence in yourself. Look for the well to fill it back in.

3. THE WAY.

Say you are stopped from doing something you have always done. Well, are you going to remain stopped? Frozen in place? Dead in the water? Be a scarecrow in the middle of the field? The choice you make is completely a personal one. But let me tell you, dying on the vine isn't as simple as it sounds. I promise that doing something, anything, is better in the long run-better for life, love, and pleasure. If you can, you find another way of getting the job done, another method of approach, an alternatives technique, and other options. If you are going deaf, you learn American sign language. Physically handicapped? Substitute card playing for sports. Can no longer see print? The other ways to read are with talking books or e-texts on a book reader or computer. The third trick to handling a disability is to find another way to do old activities. It is all about finding alternatives.

4. THE WISDOM.

In my book, the essence of wisdom lies in a person's view of life. We know that physical health is supported by positive attitudes and a cheerful disposition. Knowing these things cannot obscure the horrible depressions and rages that come with the onset of a disability, a divorce, or losing a job. We may begin with denying our condition, become intensely angry about it in the second response, and so forth, but eventually we'll bargain with God or our doctors to take it away. What could be more natural than to do as I did? After a thorough examination of my arthritis by the world-famous physician Dr. Charley Smyth, at Denver General Hospital, he asked me what I expected from treatment. I said, "A cure." He and his assistants just laughed.

Wisdom lies in the ability to come back from a

disappointment. When you step from dockside into a small boat or canoe, sometimes it rocks dangerously. The trick is to settle it back into stability. We can do that for ourselves when we know, and know deeply in our hearts, that our positive outlook on our troubles will return. We retain our strong morale despite the trouble we face. That is wisdom.

BEACH REFLECTION NO. 11

Of all the pleasures beaches offer, two are especially colorful, even desperately attractive: campfires and driving.

Take campfires. Washington beaches feature constant wind. Fires are difficult to start and often unpleasant to maintain. Smoke follows wherever you sit. Wind blows off hats and grates sand against your face. Nonetheless, flames danced beautifully in the sandy and log-strewn beachscape. And soon the shore is washed clean of ashes and embers.

As to driving on the beach, this beachcomber simply does not understand people who take their expensive vehicles onto salt-laden and wet seashores. He asked himself many times how a car's passengers could experience the charms of wave and sand and salt breeze in the glassed-in box of a car. What was the point?

Even more importantly, why cannot there be one place where cars do not go? Aren't beaches for combing, walking vigorously, or sauntering idly? Don't we wish to sit quietly to absorb the smells, sounds, and sensations of a most remarkable place?

A blind person dislikes dodging traffic in town, much less on his open beach. So many a winter day he dragged every log within two hundred yards of one point to block the beach from water to dune. He hoped the barrier would discourage drivers. He had the will, the well, the way, and the wisdom to act, quixotic as it may have seemed to anyone else.

HAIKU NO. 9

Streams of saltwater
wear across the ebb tide beach
wrinkling an old face.

CHAPTER 12

How the Four *W*s Act in Practice

1. WILLPOWER AND THE LONG ATTACK OF ARTHRITIS

A DISABILITY DOESN'T HIT ONCE, make a person adjust for once and all and then it is over. Again and again a new stage of development hits. Again and again we deny or refuse to face the change. Anger swamps our reason. We will do anything to escape our fate. We reach for desperate medical solutions or pray urgently for divine relief. Maybe, in time, we accept the new stage and move past it to as normal a life as we can.

In my twenties, still in the grip of youth, my friends talked me into playing softball. Even with my right foot acting like a peg leg, I found that I could become a .500 hitter. That, in itself, was encouraging, despite the pain.

Of course, I couldn't run. All I could do was hobble rather more like half speed. One time at bat I hit a long drive that would have been a home run. All I could do, however, was get a double. The other team refused to let someone else run for me, even though I was obviously disabled. That is one look at willpower.

At my first college teaching job, I still used a cane to take pressure off my painful right foot. One of my students asked me if I had a wooden leg. Another aspect of disability is having to face other people's assumptions, gossips, and prejudice.

Sometimes there is medical help, if not solutions. In 1971 I had a subtalar fusion of my right ankle. That eliminated the pain along with most of the foot's ability to flex. I could give up using the cane. My doctor suggested exercise as a good way to rebuild my activity level again. Because I still denied my problem, I played a season of basketball with the faculty team. Again, I scored about a dozen points a game. That was a short honeymoon, because the main drawback was that after each game my ankle would swell so much that I had to crawl into my home from the car. My doctor said a few bad words when he learned I had taken my fused right foot back onto the basketball court. By exercise, he had meant riding a static bicycle three times a week. Such are the wages of denial.

By then the arthritis had spread to my right knee. It wasn't long before I had an operation on my knee. As the years rolled on, every joint in my body became arthritic, and my medicines eventually joined with high blood pressure to damage my kidneys.

Over and over again I cycled from loss, to despair, to seeking impossible solutions, and, in between cycles, finding temporary acceptance.

During the first several decades, I still had not understood I was embarked on a life that would be defined by that cycle. In other words, will alone isn't enough by which to face calamities.

2. THE WELL AND HOW TO GET HELP

Between losing sports, living with pain, and going blind, there is not much to do besides adjust. While it is true that any of these can crash a person into despair, most of us cannot rest there. Something drives us out. Perhaps the necessity of doing something, anything, drives us; maybe frustration over what we are not doing creates enough energy for exertion; maybe friends just won't leave us alone. Something like the will arises, and we begin to look around.

In time, we buy tools to open difficult lids, plan travel so as to reduce walking distance and avoid standing for long periods; and work closely with doctors to manage the disease and keep pain under control as much as possible. Many people do these things. But where do they get the information about such tools?

When your vision is severely limited or blank, how does one cut equal pieces of pie, cake, oranges, or apples? No, if you've learned to handle a knife safely while sighted, those methods don't change. Answer: after nearly twenty years of blindness, I still can't cut anything evenly, though I can use a knife safely. Now the trick is to let your guests choose their piece of pie, cake, orange, or apple first.

How does a blind person fill a water glass without spilling? Answer: stick your finger down inside the glass to the level you want. Sorry, but Emily Post wasn't blind. Wash your hands first if cleanliness seems more important than dexterity. Or buy a little thingamabob that you lay over the edge of the glass that senses when the liquid nears the top. Then it buzzes ... most of the time. Well, can you carry the little jigger around wherever you go? Probably not.

How do you cook, clean, read, travel, or make babies when you're blind? For most of these, you can learn from other blind people, take training courses at blindness centers, or figure things out for yourself. As to making babies, anyone can do that in the dark.

Lucky for blind people, blindness training centers and mobility instructors offer exactly those new skills blind people need. The best part was all the new skills I learned, from how to tap with a white cane to adding magnifying and speech synthesizing software to my computers. Lucky it was for me that when the time came to move from handwriting everything to typing, I made that change; when the time came to adopt keyboarding rather than using a typewriter, I made that change; thus, when the transition to adaptive software to compensate for my blindness came, I was already a competent computer user. This demonstrated to me the value of lifelong learning.

So, to get all the way into the well, a person with a new disability needs to seek help wherever it is to be found. There are national organizations, local support groups, and experienced individuals who will gladly help. Often, relevant books and magazines are available. We can access federal and state organizations whose job is to keep us working, if a disability challenges our work.

Many of us have a hard time asking anyone for help. I actually had to take a formal class in asking for help. Stubborn independence can be carried too far. Not being able to drive, I learned to ask for rides to stores; not being able to read print, I learned to hire a reader. The well lies at the heart of all other ways of adjusting to disability.

3. THE WAY AND FINDING ALTERNATIVE TECHNIQUES

The basic definition of disability arises from an individual no longer being able to perform one or more of life's normal activities. These include driving, reading, speaking, working, or getting around on two feet. This is by no means an exhaustive list. One person I know suffers intense chronic pain, so that she can neither work nor perform most household duties, such as vacuuming or lifting her children into chairs or beds. Of necessity, she hired a house cleaner, uses a van with electric doors, and follows a rigorous program of pain management taught to her in Mayo Clinic's three-week pain management workshop. She has had to give up most of her desire to be a perfect housewife.

Most disabilities require careful management. Tools have to be where they can be found without searching. Training courses help those who are organizationally challenged. For weak hands, use a paddle-shaped jar opener. For vision problems, use raised marks on appliances and kitchen equipment. Difficulty in getting around? Find a cane, a walker, a wheelchair, or register for access van services. Can't use a telephone directory? Apply for free directory assistance. For any of a number of disabilities, get a service animal. As to this last, just b sure you get that animal from a recognized and certified training center. It is illegal to claim your animal is a service animal if it does not come from an authorized program.

The important principle is not to be stopped by the barrier, whatever it may be. There will be a way around it.

4. THE USE OF WISDOM TO MAKE RIGHT DECISIONS

The onset of disability forces us to make new decisions. A disability, by definition, prevents a person from pursuing some of the same activities he or she was able to do previously. Always, the question is, "What is next? What now?" All too often we get hung up on the dilemmas involved. A positive attitude needs encouragement from a particular set of decision-making skills.

First, we need to allow ourselves to understand who we really are and choose accordingly. Second, we have the absolute freedom to choose our own paths through life.

Let me begin with the second point. It is, after all, a pretty philosophical matter.

Whatever we inherit from our upbringing, we are born into a world, a solar system, and a galaxy billions of years old. All that preexistence makes us newcomers. The best we can do with that preexistence is to accommodate ourselves to it. A large part of our earthly environment is physically real and concrete. No opinion you may have of a wall, a door, or a tree changes those physical objects in any way. Like Gertrude Stein's famous phrase, "A rose is a rose is a rose." Physical things are themselves, primarily. We can associate a rose with romance, affection, or even a family group, as in English history, but those arise purely from our human thoughts. Objects in nature do not change because of what we think of them.

To acknowledge the distinction between our thoughts and outward reality constantly tests our learning. That testing helps to keep our ideas closer to the truth.

Take that group of people who dressed themselves in purple robes and then committed suicide. Only a deep disconnect between their ideas and reality could have allowed them to act with so much certainty about the existence of an alien spaceship hiding behind the Hale-Bopp comet. We humans have an immense ability to believe most anything without any real evidence or physical manifestations. That ability is something we should be very careful to be cautious about.

Just because things happen, it doesn't mean we understand them.

CHAPTER 13

The Underpinnings of Human Thought Leading toward Conclusions

CONSIDER AN AUTOMOBILE COLLISION. IT is an event so sudden that no one understands what is happening. Shock after shock of noise, jolting movements, and snaps of motion confuse us completely. Images race past our minds. Physical sensations overwhelm any ability to cope, to react other than at a subconscious level. For moments afterward we sit reeling from the chaos of it. Many minutes or even hours may pass before we can put all our impressions together into an understanding of what happened.

Any study of what witnesses report of an automobile accident shows how many different stories will come out of the same accident. In other words, the accident is a primary event we do not have a story about, that we have no immediate way to communicate, because it is primal, unexplainably real. What we understand later has been put together in the basic urge humans have to explain everything.

However, a big difference remains between the primal nature of the event and the making up of an explanation. We may tell our friends that we were in a car accident, but the words have almost nothing to do with the shocks and jangles of the event itself.

On a Memorial Day in 1984, my daughter and I hit a pickup truck creeping across the highway. For long moments, all I could do was stare at a glob of goo slopped against the dashboard that looked like brain tissue. My daughter sat frozen in the passenger seat. I could neither move nor think. Then my horrified trance broke under the babble of Christian prayer. Time began again, but everything thereafter is reconstructed memory. By the way, the goo turned out to be the chocolate ice cream my daughter had bought, not her brains. First is the event or existence, then there is the analysis of memory as we work toward meaning. So it is with existence of any kind.

The immediacy of the accident preceded my arrangement of it for the police report.

An excellent example of the natural human desire to find meaning in raw experience was reported by Margie Boule, in her article, "Survivor of Crash Wants the Details," in the January 26, 2010, (pages B1, B2, fourth column) of *The Oregonian*. A lot of people probably still have questions about exactly what happened on December 5, 2008, at about three thirty in the morning, near the Murray Boulevard overpass on US 26 in Beaverton. You may be one of them.

Maybe you were caught in the traffic jam that turned the eastbound lanes into a parking lot for hours that morning. Perhaps your vehicle finally crawled by the accident, and you saw the Mazda 6 and the Jetta, totaled. The Mazda was on its side. Or you may have heard about the accident that night on the news. You may have heard the story of the heroic Washington County deputy sheriff who, with three passersby who stopped to help, lifted the three-thousand-pound Mazda resting on the chest of a young woman. Her name was never released.

Her name is Mary Mullins. And she's one of the people who still wonder what happened that morning. "I have literally no memory of the actual event," Mary says today. "It's very frustrating." She's pieced together some accounts. "But I like my puzzles to have all the pieces," she says. No one has any doubt that the accident happened. Certainly, the woman involved, who has spent a great deal of time recuperating, has no doubt the accident happened. The event existed. Yet her greatest wish is to sort it into a memory, into an explanation, an explanation she could use to reorient herself to what is at least in part only a version of the event. The version may have little actual veracity, since it would be a reconstruction of several different sources, all varied and even sometimes contradictory, as are all eyewitness reports. All of us try for what we think of as truth, but we can only approximate the reality of the event itself. Truth lies only in the existence of the event itself, untranslatable and raw. That is why it is essential to distinguish between existence and meaning.

Start by understanding that human beings have created what we think we know. The first thing any of us needs to grasp before any other knowledge is that we humans are newcomers on earth. Let's face the fact that conclusions themselves only arrived when we humans grew into the minds we currently possess. No one knows exactly when that occurred, but the only evidence we've been able to discover argues that we existed as we are for only a blink of the time the Earth has whirled in its orbit about the sun. Neither our shared knowledge nor conclusions existed before that time.

Thus, I consider all my explanations as equally tentative, as just the best I can do with the information at hand. In plain terms, my memory supplied a version of my collision with the pickup. Memories are well-known to be error-ridden, but I feel sure that I can describe the event accurately. Aren't we all sure of our memories? We proceeded along a straight stretch of the highway, when a pickup began slowly, creepingly, across the highway from one dirt side road to another. In a glance I tried to decide whether the oncoming lane of highway was clear, so I could pass behind the pickup. But I couldn't be sure of that as I pressed the brakes. Therefore, after a hundred feet or so, the left front of my car hit the right front of the pickup, now in my westbound lane. We rolled ahead and entered the bar ditch, where we stopped. Later, I saw that the pickup had spun around to face the way it had come. Also, I remember the pickup's driver coming to my window to ask me how we were. All I remember is that my answer was unfriendly. Vaguely, it seems he explained that as he was intoxicated, he was using back roads to go home, so he wouldn't have to risk the highway. Need I say how I felt about that?

Memories alone rarely constitute a solid basis for conclusions. When the issue is important, we must verify our experience, for the experience is primal, and our conclusions are based only on afterthoughts.

We are born to a world that seems to demand that we accept sets of beliefs already laid out for us. Every college teacher knows how surprised students are when for the first time in their experience in classrooms they are sincerely being asked to think for themselves. Yet the quickest path to alienation and confusion is to try to live by someone else's beliefs, values, and style of life.

In one such class, an Honors Literature class, we studied Cooper's novel *The Last of the Mohicans*. I asked the students to tell me what they thought of the novel. One student raised his hand and went on to damn the novel as utter nonsense. Of course, I've decided not to use his own words, since some of them would be offensive. When he finished, he paused and asked in a more tentative manner, "Is it all right if I say those things?" It soon came out that he thought he was required to like any assignments a professor might require. It took me some time to convince him that to dislike an assignment was quite all right, but that I expected him to mount a rational defense.

Everyone has opinions and a complete right to have them; but opinions are of little value if the possessor cannot justify them. Our task is to examine all our societies offer up to us and find our own way of being.

That is why we have complete freedom to come to our own conclusions without bowing to any external authorities.

BEACH REFLECTION NO. 12

On several breezy and chilly days, the man wore his rubberized pants. Then he left his chair to sit among the beds of stones scattered here and there. He would gather a handful and rub them to clean off the sand. Then, if they were especially smooth, or colorful-he liked the white quartz or yellow quartz best-he would slip them into a coat pocket.

Once in a while he found some with white stripes across a black surface, or red or green stones, rarest of all.

After some hours, he would rise, collapse his canvas chair, and walk back to his little home. There he set up his rock tumbler for another five-week cycle of polishing. When at last he washed off the final polishing compound, the stones gleamed with beauty. Polishing was his way to clean the rock's window, so as to reveal God's beauty therein.

HAIKU NO. 10

Where wind whispers sand
over washed-up logs and shells,
footprints slowly fade.

PART 3

Life while Blind

BEACH REFLECTION NO. 13

The beachcomber lived alone for twelve years, shopping, cooking, cleaning, traveling, and taking care of his own business matters. Most days he hung his canvas chair over his shoulder, took up his white cane, and walked a third of a mile to the beach. In those days he had enough vision to spot his return path back up the dune. Between his beach and his home, life was good.

Then one weekend his cousin, wife, and child came to visit. To his great dismay, they would not let him near his own kitchen to cook meals for them. His cousin's wife ordered him out so she could take over. As the day passed, he watched her grow more and more tense. Soon, she began to experience nausea. She ordered her husband to take over the kitchen while she went to the bedroom to lie down. From there, she continued to issue orders.

At this point, the beachcomber decided to take his daily walk to the beach. After all, his guests were otherwise occupied. Halfway there, he discovered that they had sent their son after him. Clearly, they couldn't imagine him walking to the beach alone.

As he set his chair down in the sand and laid his white cane beside it, he wondered again what people thought he did when they weren't with him. His house was neat enough. His cousin knew he went to the beach often. He had been blind a long time, and he had seen the many ways people responded to others' disabilities. Still, it was different to have it come from family. He knew their caretaking reaction was common enough. It is so hard for sighted people to imagine being able to do anything if they were, themselves, blind.

Well, he could take it for a weekend. Gradually, his sense of loss became immersed in surf, shore, and the crisp brush of wind.

HAIKU NO. 11

A bikini-clad
woman braved the chilly beach.
Did she warm the breeze?

CHAPTER 14

Introduction to Life as a Blind Person

PICTURE ZEUS GRIPPING A FISTFUL of lightning bolts. Maybe even he wonders where and when they will strike. Similarly, a newly blinded person grips a fistful of electrical bolts that shock every part of his life, work, play, travel, shopping, marriage, reading, writing, you name it. You even identify your new post office box by location, not number. You figure out a new way to color coordinate your clothes. You buy only white cotton socks so you do not have to worry about matching them. Then, of all things, you reveal yourself to everyone else by adopting the use of a long, white cane. What a pity, people think, that a formerly capable person has lost his way. The lucky thing for Zeus is that his thunderbolts hit everyone but himself.

Adult onset blindness often creeps up gradually. Any major physical condition can begin it, whether diabetes, congestive heart disease, lupus, or even automobile accidents. Mine grew out of Crohn's disease, an inflammation of the colon. As a disease it brings along a couple of extra little goodies: arthritis and eye inflammations. Most of my adult life I could see just fine with either contact lenses or glasses. By the time my vision narrowed and decentralized, I began to lose the easy affability with the reading and writing required of a college English professor. Still, no one could look at me and say, "Wow! He's going blind." I just did not look it. After twenty-some years of increasing blindness, I still don't look blind. There is part of the problem.

Take the word "blindness," for example. How thoroughly drenched English is in the word "blind." Phrases such as, "Don't be so blind," or "He was blind to the consequences," or "He was blinded by his own fears," or "He found himself in a blind alley." The landscape of our speech. From "duck blind" to "stone blind," each involves a mess of negative for the word "blind." There is "blind man's buff" and blinds for windows and blind copy in e-mail applications. My father, who enjoyed puns, liked to repeat the sentence, "'I see,' said the blind carpenter, as he picked up his hammer and saw." Jokes aside, the most common use of the word "blind" is to indicate anything from missing the point to purposely refusing to understand. It's just about as hard to deal with the negative meanings of the word as it is to be, actually, blind.

To live blind forces one to learn a whole new set of skills. New skills appear at home, in public, and at work. Many necessary changes are all too visible to others. In public, a blind person either walks about tapping with a long white cane or by using a guide dog. Some people use both. The cane and dog also go to work, but work is where changes more economic than personal show up. The blind person needs a more expensive computer, because it must support voice recognition and/or magnification software. Many of us need a scanner to read essential print material, as well as a selection of recorders, and even a Braille typewriter. More than once other workers have expressed jealousy at my fine collection of adaptive equipment. It does not help to tell them that they, too, can get such equipment. All they have to do is go blind. I simply could not have worked without the special equipment that accommodated my needs.

When my blindness first passed into the legal definition called "legally blind," sometimes I would pass by a person who would say, loudly, "You aren't blind." Of course, I did have some vision. However, I did not have enough eyesight to travel the streets safely. With neither forward vision nor any peripheral vision in my right eye at that time, I would have been completely unsafe without my white cane. The cane identified curbs, posts, and other barriers, but even more importantly, the presence of the cane alerted pedestrians and drivers that I was visually impaired. Safety was always the overriding issue.

People's comments were not the only social issues. Whether you are different racially, ethnically, or sexually from those around you, your differences identify you with a group. Being blind puts you into one such group. In my skills training and social experience, I found I was considered as a representative of the class of people who are blind. Thus, if I made a smart remark back to the man who accused me of not being blind, he would conclude that blind people had a chip on their shoulders. I had to learn to ignore or to turn such comments into humor.

Once I went to a meeting at an elementary school

with a blind colleague who happened to have two prosthetic eyes. A student stepped in our way and said to her, "You aren't blind." She decided to just pass by without comment. To me, she said, "Boy was I tempted to pop out my prosthetics. I would have if I wasn't afraid I'd drop them on the pavement."

To this day I have never met anyone who pretended to be blind. In the land of eyes, there is nothing to be gained by not being able to see to read print, to drive a car, to wink at an attractive person, or read to your children. It is much more common to pretend more vision than you have. My father pretended he did not need reading glasses. He had no answer when I pointed out that no optometrist would have provided glasses if he did not need them.

Whatever our differences from the mob around us, we all wish to be normal. When I adopted the use of the white cane, I stopped being normal. A man would stop me in the middle of the intersection with an offer to help me cross. I confess wondering how he thought I got so far into the middle of the city. As I searched for a particular storefront, a woman far down the block called out frantically, "I'm coming!" Luckily, I escaped into the bakery before she arrived. As I passed in front of Francisco's Restaurant, I noticed a family where the parents pulled their three children tightly against the wall. I felt like joining them for a moment and then asking, "Why are we doing this?" Instead, I just tapped on past as if nothing weird was going on.

Despite even encountering people who had no idea what a white cane was or what it meant to use one, I used it to travel safely through airports, many different cities, trains and buses, and country roads. I got used to finding curiosity, skepticism, and even pity. The main thing is that I traveled safely in all these locales.

HAIKU NO. 12

When Fall dries the leaves
that drop like aged, wrinkled hands,
what is left but love.

CHAPTER 15

Workplace Discrimination

I HAVE ENDLESS STORIES ABOUT good and bad doctors, weird or nice people, strange incidents, and amazing grace. Disability is a rich tapestry but is only a part of a person's total and rich pageantry of life.

So what is disability like? It is a damned nuisance. Without doubt life would be better without it. Better, yes, but also simpler, less compromising, and less distracting. But disability is still just a nuisance. That, however, is not how "normal" people view it.

No one expects the word nuisance for a disability. People want to call it "tragic" and the disabled person "courageous." I would be courageous had I chosen to be blind. Also stupid. Tragic had I done something irretrievable from willfulness or pride. I would be tragic had I caused my own downfall through a fault of my own. Since neither arthritis nor blindness happened that way, I am neither courageous nor tragic. Nor is any other person who has a disability.

It always startled me when an acquaintance would privately express sorrow over my blindness. After the beginning of one of my courses, an older student came to me after class. After I explained how my blindness happened, she began to cry. She said, "It's so terrible that an energetic and intelligent man like you should have to be blind." I found myself telling her it was all right; I was fine with it. It seemed odd to have to comfort her. Maybe it was terrible, but my job was to get on with life. From that viewpoint, the feeling filled me that this woman had erected a barrier between us. She just had to see me as a disabled person, not a well-educated, dedicated parent and teaching professional who enjoyed people and laughter. She was, in fact, incapable of seeing me, the me who was everything else in spades and having a disability a club in a deck full of hearts. Let us pass over her explicit flattery to see the real meaning behind either pity or flattery. We may have to cope with a damned nuisance, but we are still all we ever were.

You see, blindness was not me. It was only something I had to manage, to adjust to. I felt neither less intelligent nor less capable as a professor. Using alternative methods, I could still do my job well and enjoy life thoroughly. I dealt better with blindness than with the dandelions in my lawn; better at grading papers than keeping my car washed; and I understood people better by hearing them than by seeing them. My personal identity was unaffected by either blindness or arthritis. With Popeye the sailor man I could say, "I yam what I yam, and that's all what I yam." What no disabled person can deal with is pity. No emotion is more divisive.

To deal with blindness only took a small part of a day dominated by teaching, grading papers, advising students, and serving on faculty committees. At home, it was all family, dinner prep, helping the kids with homework, and putting them to bed with love. Life for everyone is multidimensional. Pity creates a two-valued orientation of them and us, normals versus disabled, winners from down-and-outers, and the strong over the weak. Oh, the disabled, the down-and-outers, the losers, and the crips are to be pitied, are to receive charity to be lucky to receive condescending assistance, best done through the intervening structure of a charitable organization, of course, but they are not to be embraced, enjoyed, or offered the respect of active listening. Them and us does not go away until them becomes us. That is why many of us who have a disability refer to "normal" people as "temporarily able-bodied" or TABS.

Cultural prejudices of this type lay behind why I was not able to convince my English Department colleagues that my encroaching blindness left my identity unchanged. For one thing, the chairman began to make decisions for me. That had never happened before. Ordinarily, we all submitted the list of courses we wished to teach in the subsequent year. When I noticed I had not been asked for mine, I went to see the chairman. He told me they chose classes they thought I would be able to teach, given my encroaching blindness. I then made it clear that I demanded to make my own choices as usual. Later, I asked why I was not given the committee assignment I asked for. The chairman told me he thought there was too much reading involved. My explanation of how I would cope with the reading did not influence him to change his decision. In the meantime, the other members of the department got their choices. After a series of such incidents, I asked in a department meeting whether they would like me to exchange positions with a well-known member of the Marketing Department. I said that despite his reputation as a poor teacher who read to his students from the textbook, he had perfectly good eyesight. They could, then, have a colleague who was a poor teacher with good eyes instead of a good teacher with bad eyes. They neither saw the humor nor the point. Then I was passed over when it came my turn to be department chairman.

Obviously, one reason disability is a nuisance is that people discriminate against you. Certainly they do it from ignorance, for the most part. Sometimes they refuse to acknowledge their own revulsion about the condition. But the fear of it blocks understanding and even civil attempts at courtesy. They tell themselves they are only being helpful.

As time went by, I discovered that some students were being warned off my classes because I was going blind. Naturally, I had to learn many new skills to keep teaching. I hired a person to read student assignments to me while I dictated comments and grades. I began to have assignments come in on computer disks so I could read them with my computer's speech synthesizer. I read the books I assigned in talking book formats. I was, after all, a dedicated teacher and desired to continue to teach effectively. It really hurt to have colleagues talking me down behind my back.

With everything else going downhill, I began a dialog in department meetings about discrimination. I saw immediately that no one understood what constituted discrimination. That is the problem with white privilege. One does not even notice the privilege. It just seems to be the normal condition of life for those who have it. I had lost it by going blind, and they could not grasp how a blind person could be as good a teacher as a sighted person, however bumbling that sighted person may be.

Finally, I decided I had to retire to seek a new career. At that same time, the department hired an African American professor. She asked my assistance with the department, as she faced the racial discrimination of which they seemed so pointed and yet so unaware. I made no more progress with them on her behalf than I had on my own.

Thus I learned that discrimination hurts everybody. Those who cannot see it likely never will. If they don't experience it themselves, they cannot encompass it. Therefore, for them it does not exist.

BEACH REFLECTION NO. 14

Oh, how the heavy seas rearranged the furniture of the beachscape! Each time he slipped down the last dune onto the level sand, he found every landmark he'd noted had either moved or disappeared.

His biggest surprise came when a three-trunked and nine-foot root mass had obviously been washed away. He had never seen anything bigger on the shore than that. Now it was gone.

For a time, a few logs placed strategically before the place where he descended to the beach had guided him back from his walks with his guide dog up one direction and down the other before returning to his points of reference. Suddenly, those were gone, and the beach was bare of driftwood. How, then, could he tell where to find his path back to his house?

The shore changed endlessly, as his own life had changed endlessly, whether he liked it or not. When life was good, it got worse; when it felt worse, change to good. He always felt that each would last. They never did. To tell the truth, as much as his experience of the beach verified his experience of life, he never quite got rid of his belief in stability. Some knowledge is hard to move from the intellectual to the realistic. All he knew was that time spent rock hunting on the shore helped him with coming back to realism.

HAIKU NO. 13

What she said was true:
C Dog danced his way through life,
every path a gift.

CHAPTER 16

My Wonderful Guide Dog, Commodore

ONE DAY COMMODORE AND I walked toward a corner where we usually crossed on our way to the bus stop. The road I followed went straight on, but there was an intersection for the "T," or turn to my right. I could hear a truck rattling toward us. As it began its turn into the "T," I also heard the rattle of a trailer. Suddenly the truck stopped, then began to back up. This I could hear, but presumed the driver would back the trailer into the street along which I walked. Thus, I kept walking toward the corner. When Commodore stopped and began to back up swiftly, something he had never done before, I felt bewildered. Yet I walked backward with him. With my limited vision, I suddenly realized the truck's trailer had backed across the sidewalk in front of me and nearly struck the fence at the corner. I could tell, vaguely, that long poles or two-by-fours projected out beyond the trailer. Then the truck pulled forward and went back the way it had come. Had Commodore not pulled me back, I could have been seriously injured by a driver who made a serious driving error. He clearly didn't know or care how to back a trailer properly. It also seemed clear he never saw me. My old white cane would never have protected me in this situation.

Guide Dogs for the Blind, in Boring, Oregon, paid my airfare. Their representative picked me up at the airport and drove me to the campus. For two days a trainer led me about to see how fast I walked, how well I took directions, and how well I responded to corrections. On the third day, they sat me on a couch in the training supervisor's office. Then, finally, stunningly, they brought in a three-year-old yellow Lab and golden retriever cross named Commodore. Commodore was, and is, my first guide dog for the blind.

A first guide dog must be a stunning experience for every blind person who gets one. I could hardly breathe. I certainly was unable to apply the discipline of handling him they had already begun to teach me. All I wished was to hug him, pet him, and celebrate him. A very distant background noise kept telling me to control my dog. At that moment of meeting Commodore, I could do nothing but gaze at him in wonder. That is how it began for me at the Boring, Oregon, campus of Guide Dogs for the Blind.

Before I go on to tell about my guide dog, let me say that Guide Dogs for the Blind is the most effective organization I have ever experienced. That includes five universities and two government departments. Their kennel houses about 175 dogs in clean conditions wherein the animals are beloved. The facility is complete and expertly groomed. The staff works together to cook excellent food, serve the food efficiently, and care for all activities in a fully cooperative spirit. They give the dogs training in all the conditions they will meet in the world. Their commitment to safety could teach all of us how to live. All this work, preparation, dog breeding, and training comes at no cost to the blind person. But, finally, the main fact of all is this: they handed me Commodore. I think there was a floor under my feet as I walked Commodore on leash back to my room. As instructed, I brought him to his corner of the room, where I had placed his mat. Then I sat on the bed to just look at him.

The first thing I noticed was the look he had of being concerned. The effect arose from his eyes. Set in a sort of triangle, his eyes were a warm brown. When I spoke to him, he raised his brows. His long, floppy, and silky ears lifted. He did not lie down but sat still, with eyes shifting from me to the door. As I talked reassurances to him, petted him, and so forth, it struck me what a shock it must be for him to move out of the kennel, away from the familiar dogs there, away from his handlers and trainers, and be brought to a strange room in which sat a stranger. It seemed obvious that it would take a long time to create a bond with him, just as the trainers had told me. That was just the third day of my four weeks of training with Commodore.

We arose at six in the morning, dressed, relieved the dog, ate breakfast, and started class at eight in the morning. Relieve the dog again at nine and noon. With the exception of a lunch break, classes went until four or four thirty in the afternoon. Relieve the dog. Eat dinner. Back in class until nine. Relieve the dog and go to bed. We did that schedule six days a week, around campus, on the streets in Gresham, across parks, and along country roads. We called it guide dog boot camp. Mind you, it wasn't Commodore being trained, it was me. Like most people, I knew nothing about handling a dog, let alone how to turn my entire mobility over to a guide dog.

The word "blind" in common usage refers to a visual acuity of 20/200 or beyond, even with corrective lenses. For day-to-day meaning, to be blind is to be unable to read newsprint or other types of print even with glasses. Only about 15 percent of people called blind are completely without vision. Yet many people still associate the word with complete darkness. The fact is that most people who are classified as blind have some amount of vision; enough, say, to navigate in buildings or streets during daytime. Still, with limited vision they are probably not safe while crossing streets or facing unexpected barriers. That is why, in 1988, I adopted a white cane.

Why didn't I just go ahead to get a guide dog? Another fact is you cannot get a guide dog until you have learned mobility skills with a white cane. White cane skills are a prerequisite. Even more, I liked the white cane for years. I got around well. I felt safe until certain situations made cane use difficult. At night, on some residential streets, I found the erratic placement of poles, curb cuts and broken sidewalks tiring. My cane would catch in holes or miss a pole, which I would step into or run against. At night, the dark road I traveled to get home from the bus had no sidewalk, as happens in many remote areas. I could not tell where the pavement ended and the bar ditch began. I fell.

Such incidents began to make me feel that I needed a better way to get around safely. It's hard enough for a blind person to take up a white cane. People truly do look at you differently. One of my blind friends asked me the right question: "Would you rather be thought stupid when you run into a wall, or smart when you cane around it?" It is true that a skilled cane user gives a better impression than a stumbling Mr. Magoo. Besides, you don't have to feed a white cane, groom it, or make sure it gets enough exercise and attention. A guide dog requires much more maintenance than a white cane. So I went on well for those years until I began to find the cane to be a lot of effort, yet still led me into mistakes.

It is also no coincidence that my vision deteriorated all through those years. I became less and less self-confident. So I decided to get a guide dog. Here's the thing, a dog walks right past the poles you used to have to find with a cane. You don't even have to know they exist. A dog stops at every curb, at once stopping you from stepping off into space, unprepared, and also informing you that you have walked another block. All mobility decisions are still yours. The dog doesn't know whether you want to turn left or turn right or go forward. You still have to know where you are going. Therein lies the necessity of having good blindness-related mobility skills. The dog will avoid moving automobiles, pedestrians, and other objects along the particular pathway. You don't have to find them by tapping along with your white cane. Much easier.

Whether to use a white cane permanently or get a guide dog is a personal decision. Most blind people stay with the cane. It fits into cars better. No one is allergic to canes, and no one worries about getting cane hair on their clothes. Wipe them down with a damp cloth, and you are off to wherever you want to go. The purposes of both the white cane and the guide dog are the same. Both enhance the safety of the blind person. Even more, both help the blind person to be independent. It is basic to life to be able to freely come and go, to shop and walk, to visit and work, to meet and greet, to cook and clean. Mobility is the basic freedom. Whether one achieves freedom with a white cane or a guide dog is immaterial.

Back to Commodore. I will not apologize for saying that he's the brightest and most intelligent dog there is, except possibly for Tippi, my friend's guide dog. Anyone would be amazed to watch Commodore glide through the masses of people, benches, and hallway displays in a shopping mall. He plans his route through the mess so smoothly I wouldn't have to know others were standing or walking around. He also gives a little jig to the harness each time we pass a doorway into a shop. Thus, I can even count the stores to find the one I'm looking for. He stops at the top or bottom first step of any stairway until I find it with my toes. He stops and goes on command. When a route becomes familiar, he just goes as I wish. If I am inside a store and the outside door is visible to him, I just command, "Commodore, find outside." Out we go.

My white cane could never get me outside unless I knew the way. Some stores design their aisles so a person has to be an intelligent rat to find the path to the outside door. I think we all know which stores I mean. We all know that dogs act with more responsiveness to humans and their activities than other domestic animals. Thus, I don't need to explain how swell a partner Commodore was during my years of living alone. Every care I lavished on him came back with interest as I fumbled with relationships, tried to find work I could still do, and travel to see family and friends.

As I write, he sits by me on the love seat. We are close, close. But all animals comfort and support us in one way or another. Anyone may wonder what is so special, then, about guide dogs. First, they undergo lifelong training. Selected carefully even as puppies, they must have no physical defects of any kind. They cannot be overly aggressive or too passive. They must show immediate interest in their surroundings and in being handled. After that, they are run through training courses to determine balance and agility, intelligence and cooperativeness. Then volunteers agree to raise the dogs for basic commands and obedience, while exposing them to every situation life affords. I like to think of this as their version of a bachelor's degree. As such degrees do, such training sharpens their intelligence and confidence.

Most people don't know that some months after their first year, they are brought to the guide school for the specific training in guiding human beings safely through whatever barriers, hazards, or routes are faced by their blind person. This training lasts approximately six months and is reinforced during the time they wait to meet the blind person with whom they will be bonded. That day is called graduation, and I consider it their doctorate. By now their intelligence has been enhanced to nearly the degree possible to each of them in their different ways. In case any self-righteous person thinks of guide dogs as enslaved or forced into guide behavior, let them alleviate their ignorance for themselves by studying books dedicated to explaining the dog's mind. Guide dogs love their work. They come eagerly to the harness and eagerly strut along the streets into stores, proud of their work. After all, the safety of their human is in their hands, or paws, to be less metaphorical. Their reward is our appreciation, our praise, and the offer of a kibble for a special success.

I don't wish to exaggerate my love for Commodore. Once I knew a family who loved their dog so much they thought it was cute when he pooped on the floor. They chuckled with enjoyment when he persistently kept trying to hump a dog guest. No, I give Commodore the same affection I give my family, and work to help him with his weaknesses. He loves people too much and bounces crazily when a person comes to the door. Those moments take a lot of restraint. I've watched him flirt with other customers in a coffee shop or nearby passengers on a bus. They don't seem able to resist those warm brown eyes with that triangular twinkle. Yes, he has faults. On the other hand, he has saved me from injury several times.

One day I walked on my usual route to a grocery store. I paused at the usual corner and the usual light. When I heard the cars stop at the light, I gave Commodore the order to go forward. He refused. He didn't move. This was very unusual. No one who has never had a guide dog could appreciate how unusual was his refusal. Guide dog trainers say one of the hardest aspects of training a dog is to teach the animal when to disobey. A normal dog's temperament lies in granting authority to the alpha dog. Blind masters are taught to act as alpha dogs. I knew this and asked Commodore to go forward, again. He did not move. I kept puzzling over it until a passerby spoke to me. "I wouldn't have believed it if I had not seen it," he said. "There's a three-foot trench in front of you. Your dog kept you from falling into it." Mind you, it would have been better for the road construction gang to have placed barriers in front of their trench. Since they had not, this is one of the times that Commodore got his kudos, and we took an alternate route. Nor was his behavior unusual.

He always stops at barriers. We've often encountered cars parked across sidewalks, construction sawhorses blocking our route, or sidewalks ending abruptly in underdeveloped residential areas. He has stopped me when cars cut a corner to pass in front of us or when a car attempted to zoom out of a driveway without looking for pedestrians. One common danger is the free right turn on red lights. Consider the situation. If traffic is approaching from the left and the driver wants to turn right onto that road, which way is he looking? Left, of course. Where is the blind pedestrian? To the driver's right, of course. Commodore has stopped me many a time when the driver began to move through the crosswalk. Good job, Commodore.

I think his most significant rescue of me was a situation I could not either grasp or foresee. You never know what stupid action a driver may attempt. Thus I know how deeply I am indebted to Commodore and to Guide Dogs for the Blind who trained him in his excellent skills. A partner who keeps you independent and also safe is a valuable partner, indeed. Think what I would have missed had I not chosen positively during my nearly annual declines in vision. Not only would I have never met and loved Commodore, never have experienced the liberty he gave me, never have kept working, for that matter, or never have kept an active and fulfilled life.

EPITAPH

Commodore, 5/26/2000–1/9/2013

May he meet his maker with the same joyful
steps with which he danced through life.

BEACH REFLECTION NO. 15

He went to bed with the sound of surf rumbling
softly through his bedroom window. He rose to
surf sounds around his morning coffee. Some days

a quiet surf whispered over the dunes between his house and the shore fifteen hundred feet away. Other days, whipped by a storm, winds blew the thunder of each wave dropping heavily onto the sand. No two days sounded the same, but life was measured by surf.

On days of warm sun, he sat on the front deck and marveled at how the distant roar would seem to come only from the south. Or it emanated from the north. Rarely did the sound seem to roll straight toward him. Yet straight ahead lay the nearest path to the water. How the sound constantly moved from south to north always amazed him. Was it the direction of the wind that controlled the direction of surf sounds? Did surf sometimes pound more solidly in some areas than others? Did it matter whether there was incoming or outgoing tide?

He did not know the answer. For some crazy reason, it pleased him that he did not know. While sitting on his warm deck, reflecting on the nature of things came naturally. This reflection made him realize that many people hated not knowing. It made them grasp with certainty at beliefs that themselves were open to question. He had often heard that it was a characteristic of creative people that they were comfortable with ambiguity. Maybe that was true for intelligent or enlightened people generally. Maybe.

He, himself, was so comfortable with the ambiguity of the direction of surf sounds that he laid his head back and fell asleep in the sun.

HAIKU NO. 14

The two-track road leads
to a lone stand of piñons.
A whippoorwill sings.

CHAPTER 17

Camping while Blind, or "CWB"

NOW LET ME TAKE UP the first point about the real basis of personal wisdom. First, we need to allow ourselves to understand who we really are and choose accordingly.

For this, I am going to tell the story of my solo camping trip at Navaho Lake during springtime in the Rockies. The story dramatizes the problems inherent in personal decision making, especially as they relate to disability.

My camp was set along the shore of Navaho Reservoir on a sandstone shelf fronting a copse of pinion pines. First, let me go back to putting up the tent. That is a way more difficult task for a guy with bad eyes. The Coleman "Oasis" features spring-loaded upright poles that must be inserted into the right lengths of poles topped by a plastic insert. That insert has to fit into crosspieces that tighten both side rooms and a long ridgepole that also spreads awnings over doors on each side of the tent. The ridgepole contains four or five pieces, I don't remember exactly how many, but they have to be exactly right to stretch and hold the ridge in place. The uprights that hold up the ridge have at least three pieces and raise the ridge to nine feet. Each of the many pieces are printed in black ink to identify them.

One definition of a legally blind person is that he cannot read print. So how did I put the pieces together? I did not do it by reading the labels and assembling the pieces accordingly. Instead, I sat on the ground and put like with like. One group had plastic nipples, some yellow and a few orange. Another group contained springs. These would snap to the shorter, nippled poles to create the uprights that lifted each far end of the tent. Another set had plastic blue rings at each end. These would fit together to stretch the tent between the uprights. How could I go wrong when I understood what each piece was meant to do? We all have five senses, not just one. Vision is wonderful, very dominant to most people, but I would rather use my sense of taste for food, my sense of touch for lovemaking, and my hearing to know what Caliente is doing and where he is when out of sight. To explain, I understand my tent, and by feel I can put the right pieces together to raise the tent.

Nothing could have felt better than to pass a few hours in the methodical ordering of a camp that suited me perfectly.

Because springtime in the Rockies is always a chancy business, I set up my camp stove inside the tent along with the ice chest and boxes of food. A camp chair finished off my dining room. Using a bellows pump, I filled a queen-sized air mattress. Now back, I zipped two heavy sleeping bags together for the bed and then threw down my pillows and extra blanket on top. Friends had commented that the bed inside the tent made my setup look like a Persian seraglio. I doubt any of them had seen such a place, but the comparison pleased me, anyway. Nothing had ever attracted me to discomfort.

That made it time to take my shovel off to establish a latrine. Now it was time to tend to Caliente. Friends had helped me to find him, a reddish quarter horse gelding often praised by my "horse people" friends as "a good-looking animal." By "horse people," I mean those so used to horses in their lives that they alternatively referred to a horse by either the rider's or horse's name without being aware of it. They would say, "There goes Gail with her tail in the air." Of course, Gail was the rider, not the horse. They only laughed when I pointed it out to them. "What difference does that make?" they would ask. So it pleased me that they liked the look of my horse. However, I was never a good enough rider to excite Caliente into galloping along with his tail held high. I always felt a strong desire to remain in the saddle, and in fact I never did fall off. I had tied Caliente to a long rope hobbled to a large tire. With that he could wander around the field near my camping spot to find the early grasses. I brushed him down and cleared his hooves of mud before I saddled up. I preferred the Australian saddle because my legs were weak from years of arthritis, and the saddle's flanges that held my thighs greatly assisted my ride. To protect myself from the stirrup and its leathers, I tied soccer shin guards around my shins. Sometimes disabilities require quite a bit of equipment to compensate for it. Thus attired, I mounted, and Caliente and I rode up the valley.

You may ask, and may well wish to ask, what is a visually impaired person doing riding off on a horse without a guide? Where is the helper person, where is the nurse, where is the responsible wife who should be taking care of this nearly blind and largely arthritic man as he forays into a world he can barely see? I have been asked that. I can tell that even those who didn't ask would have liked to ask.

Remember? I am camping solo. My ability to reason and use my hands to feel the nature of each piece of equipment lets me also blow up air mattresses, zip sleeping bags together, and use a camp stove and cookware. No doubt I could do most jobs more quickly were I able to read print or spot tools scattered around my tent site. However, one of the pleasures of camping alone is that I could enjoy my work without some retinal chauvinist wishing I would get it done more swiftly. In any case, most of those who looked over my tent couldn't understand how to put my poles together even though they could read the printed labels. Understanding remains more powerful than vision.

It's a somewhat different case as I rode out on Caliente. I understand that many people know little about horses. The author Barbara Cartland, for example, tells that her princess in the novel *The Proud Princess* galloped her horse across a river. Had that been a real situation, the princess's pride would have been much diminished by a complete drenching in the river. If we define a river as running more than a foot deep, no horse could gallop across it. There would be a complete and hard fall for the formerly proud princess. The one thing to know about horses is that they would rather return home than ride out. So no matter where the blind man rides, the horse returns to the feedbag every time. Also, my friends had found me a very good animal that wanted to take care of me and never brushed me off to a low-hanging branch.

I enjoyed my ride up the valley on my horse. The smell of sage, the occasional Chinese elm, or willow growing from a dry watercourse, and always I was filled and surrounded by the stimulating air of the Colorado plateau. I paused in what appeared to be a grass-filled basin where in the past someone had made an earthen dam, now gone. Caliente froze when a fast buzz or rattle sound arose from underfoot. Here again, it didn't matter whether I could see anything. Both Caliente and I knew enough to leave.

People are fond of observing to disabled people how courageous they must be. People cannot imagine what it must be like to be blind or paraplegic or weakened by multiple sclerosis. Their failure of imagination forces them to be agog at the difficulties faced by disabled people. Now, with a presumed rattlesnake warning us off, I might have been either courageous or stupid to dismount and attempt to find the snake, perhaps with the intention of killing it. I remember as an eight- or nine-year-old when a rattlesnake crossed a path in front of me. I tried to follow it into the weeds to see where it was going. It took me some moments to wake up to what I was doing. I smarted up and ran back to the path. Lucky for me, the snake didn't want anything to do with me.

In this situation, I felt no temptation to investigate. I would rather be a snake in the grass than looking for a snake in the grass. I might find it. Some would say that I was correct about the snake but showed courage by being a disabled person who would ride a horse or go camping alone. After all, most people can neither imagine being blind nor being able to do anything if they were blind. The only way I can think to help them understand is to say this: "Since you cannot imagine it, just believe the person who knows."

One of the most amazing experiences when one becomes disabled is how many people don't believe you when you tell them what it is like to be blind or paraplegic or dependent on breathing apparatus. I confess I knew nothing about blindness either until I became blind. In my early thirties, a Vietnam veteran who had been blinded by shrapnel enrolled in one of my classes. He had to teach me to speak what I wrote on the board, for example, for I was used to assuming all my students could read what I wrote on the board. He could not. He requested permission to record my class sessions. I gladly granted his request. In later years, I heard of cases where professors refused to allow disabled students to record their lectures. Perhaps karma will bring them to a suitable end. As for me, Doug, my blind Vietnam vet, found that while his instructor didn't really grasp what it was like to be blind, he did accept Doug's description of what he needed to function independently as a student. As I said, if people can't imagine a condition, they can at least accept the word of one who knows, and act accordingly. So why don't they?

There are those who cannot believe anything they cannot imagine. Say that an African American describes discrimination. These unimaginative sorts cannot believe she has been discriminated against because they have not "seen" themselves discriminated against. I tell them that, while I can no longer read print, I can access print by using someone to read to me, by using tapes, Optical Character Recognition scanners, and speech synthesizers. Because they don't understand how they could read using such alternative techniques, they don't believe me. They cannot believe what they cannot imagine.

Let them imagine me turning Caliente toward home, that is, back to camp. He knows; he knows. Yet, even with limited vision, I also know. There's the dry watercourse outlined with Chinese elm and dry willows. It lay on my left as I rode out and on my right as I ride back. Caliente stops where I saddled him; he makes me think he is much smarter than people I have described above who fail to imagine beyond their limited experience. I love this red horse. He actually has a sardonic sense of humor. He came from a family where children rode him. He used to torment them when they mounted. They would heel him to go, and he would back up. He liked that game. My horse people explained how to handle that. They said, "If he wants to back up, tighten up the reins, lean back, and make him walk back. After that, he will be happy to go when you start him. Horses generally don't like backing up. He's just learned it to torment those who let him get away with it." So the first day I mounted Caliente and gave the signal to go, he started to back up. I noticed he dropped his jaw and joked back at me—until I pulled back on the reins and leaned back in the saddle. He quickly tired of backing and willingly went forward as asked. I loved my sardonic yet completely safe animal. I brushed him down, cleaned his hooves, and carried the tack back to my camp. That was just the first day.

On my fourth day, a cold front came through the area. I woke to the sound of scratchy snow striking the tent and sliding off. Caliente rustled the shrubbery close to the tent. All else lay quiet, like the moment just before you know that something is going to happen. I opened myself to the deep stillness of nature. I lay warm and comfortable in my sleeping bags and ten-inch deep air mattress. At any moment, I could rise, fire up the camp stove, and let the tent warm. When ready, I could dress and make breakfast with hot coffee. I could stay inside to read in bed using my tape player or listen to my boombox report the weather. I could do whatever I wished. The snow was not heavy and was no threat. The cold was no bother, for I had come prepared for it. I had plenty of food and a good supply of kerosene for the camp stove. Caliente already had his winter coat, so he, too, was fully ready for rough weather. I needed only to keep camping.

As the snow continued to fall, its ticking against the tent, the branches of the pinions, and clumps of sage set up a trouble in my mind. The snow wore a place in me where a worry arose. Worry is a strange business. To me it implies being troubled about something over which you have no influence, no means of changing, to me a useless process. Yet there it was, haunting me like this: my friends are going to be especially concerned about me being alone in a snowstorm. Damn it, I am fine, but they probably are not. I have my camp, my stove, my bed, my horse, but probably all of this only increases their concern for their blind friend. They worried he couldn't cope with camping alone, so how much more will they worry that he is alone in a snowstorm? Yet I am fine. What to do?

At last I decided I must let my friends know that I was all right. I put on my warmest clothes, donned my huge yellow rain slicker, and pulled the hood over my Australian outback hat. Caliente stood quietly as I brushed him down, cleaned his hooves, and saddled him. I mounted, and we went to the two-track rough road that led back out of my remote camping spot. The tire tracks remained bare mud as snow built up on the grasses and shrubs outlining the tracks. Sometimes logic makes you go wrong in a state of great confidence. If I followed the road back, that would be the long way. The road goes, say, five miles along this hillside before it takes a U turn and runs down the other side of the hill and so out of the area.

So my thinking went like this: if I do what horses can do, I can ride over this hill and down the other side to where the road passes on the other side.

You don't have to be blind to be stupid. Logic is cold meat when it fails. I turned from the road and passed up the hillside. Caliente climbed easily. After all, where does a thousand-pound horse go? Anywhere he wants. At first, trees and a sort of openness before me gave me pleasure in the ride in and about the hillside's pinion trees. The snowfall lay lightly enough on the landscape to sculpt it in beauty but not diminish it to be threatening. As we reached what seemed to be the summit, barriers seemed to develop. Shall we turn around this outcropping? Does this narrow way between trees lead downward? The horse and I circled and searched until a moment came when Caliente would go forward no more, no matter how much I clucked or kicked heels. All right. Now the snow really fell on cedars. Coloradans often call pinions cedars for their reddish wood and cedar smell. I could smell them; I could hear snow; I could not see a way forward. My only boast is that I trusted Caliente. Earlier I said I sometimes thought he was more intelligent than those unimaginative people who won't even listen when someone who knows tells them the truth about disability. Now I began to grasp that he was more intelligent than me, by a long shot.

As I sat there, beginning to think, the area around me began to make sense. When you are visually impaired, it can take awhile to put together vague visual input to build a scene. Snowfall hindered me, so it was some time before I began to realize that Caliente and I stood poised at the top of a cliff. One more step, and we would have had a ride, for sure. I patted my horse gratefully, pulled him back from the precipice (at that moment he didn't mind backing). "By God," I told him in a loud voice, "we know how to get back down this hill, don't we?" And we did. Back on the road, Caliente's clopping added the only sounds heard over the silencing of the snowfall. It's amazing how sensible and patient you can be just after you nearly did a very stupid thing.

Occasionally we trotted, sometimes loped, but mostly just clopped along. Conditions were just too slippery for speed. By this time, my gloves were drenched. I never wanted to be a hero in a spaghetti western, and here I was, braving bad riding conditions. I would much rather have stayed in my tent-warm, dry, and well-fed. After an hour or so, we found the causeway that blocked one end of the reservoir. The wind and wind chill hit harder there, and we were glad to get across and into more hills. The road climbed into an area where a network of roads confused me. There were signs for picnic areas and camping areas, but no clear signs for the lake resort. I tried a downhill-slanting road, but without a sign, lost confidence. We went back up the road and tracked along the signs for picnicking and camping again.

Finally I gave in to the downhill road and after a twenty-minute ride finally came to the resort. That was a difficult three-hour ride. Sure enough, when I tramped down the ramp onto the barge with its resort cabin, I found my friends Denise and Bill worried and glad to see me. They are two of the best people I have ever known, so their concern touched me. They wanted to help me pack up my camp and had already arranged for the Fish and Game man there to use his boat. They had also already called my wife to bring out the truck and trailer from town. She wasn't particularly happy to have her work interrupted. So, I acquiesced.

Here is where Samuel Johnson's quotation comes in. Like many people, I would rather give than to receive assistance. The former gives control and an easy pleasure; receiving seems to leave behind obligation and a bit of guilt that one even needs assistance. Why, then, would such an accomplished and intelligent man as Johnson assert that giving and receiving assistance were the greatest pleasures? Well, helping me gave my friends great pleasure. They sincerely believed I needed help that snowy day. They believed that even after I showed up having ridden Caliente ten miles or so through bad roads and difficult tracks. Didn't that mean I was capable? Competent? Able to stand on my own two feet? I love Bill and Denise, but on that day even they did not believe me when I said there was no problem. We all crossed the lake, packed me up, and sent me home.

The next day dawned cold and clear and just right for camping and riding in the Rockies. But I was home. Let us not oversimplify my situation. Yes, of first importance is to live life on your own terms. Yes, again, the degree to which you let others direct your life is the degree to which you lose your sense of self. On the other hand, any sensible person will tell you how important it is to surround yourself with a loving and supportive circle of friends. The challenge of being an individual, the oneself, and yet being a member of the many has long been a central concern of our best literature and philosophy. We wonder how to be ourselves in addition to fitting in with the other members of a department, neighborhood, church, or community group. From this, I take it that maintaining a sense of self while engaging with others creates constant dilemmas for all of us.

You could ask, "Did Larry do wrong to give in to his friends? He wanted to stay in his camp; at the same time, he wanted to please his friends. No situation is really that simple. For instance, the wet snowfall made the track into his camp a lot muddier. To drive in with a heavy truck and horse trailer and then to add camping equipment and a thousand-pound horse could make it difficult to drive back out, four-wheel drive or not. The weather is a real factor. Another factor is that his friends had already convinced the Fish and Game officer to use his boat to go across the lake to pick up all the camping equipment. After all, he had already brought his thousand-pound horse to the resort with its paved roads. Did Larry compromise his own wishes and thus compromise his sense of self? He did feel that way, but there is always another level of thinking called good sense. By anyone's best judgment, despite a personal wish, the condition of the track into his camping spot was probably too muddy to rely on. By riding the horse out, he made a better choice possible." Many times the best decision is a validation of a sense of self that can choose the right thing rather than a personal thing that could create new difficulties. The wisest course often builds character better than a selfish choice. I helped myself that time by admitting that I had chosen to go home rather than having been forced by my friends. The funny thing is they were right.

HAIKU NO. 15

When the blind gull flies,
his heart's orientation
spins him past danger.

PART 4

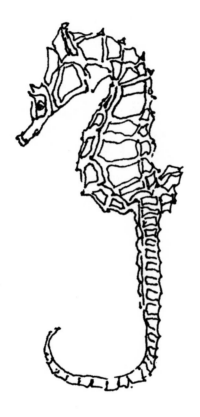

Hard Sailing toward a
Sense of Purpose

BEACH REFLECTION NO. 16

Many days on the beach held him in the thrall of memory. Perhaps it was the rhythmic spell of wave action that entranced him.

Despite the gulls and crows, or even passersby, all he could do is remember the navy destroyer that was his home. Yet it was an awkward home for him. It was a life of small metal rooms, intense crowding, and mindless routines. Breaking into these were flashes of brilliance: the exoticism of Pearl Harbor, Hong Kong, and Manila; the thrill of flying fish pulling from the sea and coasting alongside; porpoises leaping past with their flying arches; the phosphorescence of the dusky sea in the ship's wake.

Still, he was not at home in the navy. He often resented orders and the utter regimentation, and he hated the guns and gunnery practice.

One day, as he waited for a transfer back to the United States, he finally resolved his doubts. He knew, utterly and finally, that he would not reenlist. No matter its good aspects, this life was not for him.

HAIKU NO. 16

He met her surfside
untill C Dog nosed her crotch
when she nearly swooned.

CHAPTER 18

Let Each of Us Find the Purpose of Our Own Unique Lives

WE WOULD ALL PROFIT FROM taking a moment to consider an experience before coming to conclusions about it. Inattention does the most to interfere with our recognizing that we indeed act on our intuitions about what life really means to us personally. Yet, if we don't recognize our sense of personal purpose, we can be pushed this way and that into a relatively persistent confusion. If it isn't the swift pace of life, our inattention comes from dwelling on the past or feeling anxiety about something in the future. Worry can carry us for hours before we realize that worry gains us no solutions. To push worry into the space where we can deal with the issue rather than just to process it endlessly takes an exertion of will. It's better to have the habit of abiding in the present.

On the other hand, the present can occupy us to such an extent that we forget ourselves. A flurry of distractions may place us in another space, a space where we become unaware of our own consciousness. What I mean by being present is to be aware of ourselves in the present, able to decide issues by what we feel or believe.

In a philosophical sense, we live in absolute freedom to choose. However, something in our transcendent selves, those selves that partake in everything that exists, signals like an intuitive weather vane that our lives have a particular direction, a specific purpose. Something in us tells us there are certain directions that attract and others of indifference or repulsiveness. There are life directions that create a sense of well-being and others that give unease. After a time, if we try, we can find we are, ourselves, meant to teach, or build and make, or garden, play sports, or serve the public. Some of us commit to the welfare of others in an endless variety of ways. For some, the guide is to marriage and family.

Yet, if we find ourselves accurately, we can grasp that our particular way is not exactly that of anyone else. For example, there were many ways for me to be a teacher, but my own way finally was a way only I could be.

To exist in the present means both to be a whole consciousness in the present as well as contain the whole sense of the past and the future. Awareness of a personal purpose for life also sustains us through periods of crisis or conflict.

For some of us, to be present comes rarely. Our culture moves swiftly, too swiftly, we believe, to allow us time for reflection. We think we have no time to look attentively at any present moment. While driving, we make cell phone calls; while eating, we send text messages by phone; with nothing in our hands, we daydream. What a difference it makes to stop and see, see thoroughly and for a space of time before we judge or interpret or assign meaning. Most of us jump to judgment, in truth, before we really see anything.

I remember a PTA meeting where the mother of the high school's head boy and current sports hero argued that the school was pushing its students too hard. She said she wanted her son to have time to look out the window. Because she was talking about a teenager, those at the meeting had a good laugh at the idea of a teenager who never had an idle moment.

Most of us thought our teenagers took too much idle time. The truth is, though, that our reaction was just the habit of our culture to believe that idleness meant wasting time. In contrast, it is a well-established principle that idleness is an essential ingredient in both creativity and invention.

The great mathematician Henri Poincare wrote that his mathematical breakthroughs all came when he was taking a break from his work, not when he was engaged in working formulas. Examples abound that prove the value of idleness to constructive thinking.

It's natural enough to ask ourselves, "Why am I here?" One of my students mocked my emphasis on that existential question by laying a bent-up piece of paper clip on my desk. I didn't get it, to my shame. I asked him what it meant, and he said, "Wire we here?" All joking aside, "Wire we here?" is the question, but it has a personal answer for each of us.

No book I know has more power to illustrate how important it is for us to keep our sense of purpose alive in each present moment than Victor Frankel's book *Man's Search for Meaning*. Frankel was already a doctor and psychiatrist when the Germans sent him to one of their death camps in World War II. He endured and survived, and he used what he learned to create a process of therapy he called logo therapy, or more commonly known today as cognitive therapy. Here is one of the significant passages where he passes along some of his important realizations about living by a personal sense of self and being rooted in the present moment.

Near the end of the war, all those in the camp who still survived planned escape...Suddenly I decided to take fate into my own hands for once. I ran out of the hut and told my friend that I could not go with him. As soon as I had told him with finality that I had made up my mind to stay with my patients, the unhappy feeling left me. I did not know what the following days would bring, but I had gained an inward peace that I had never experienced before.

Frankel explains that the only way camp inmates could stay sane was to hold on to their own sense of the purpose of their lives. In a real sense, he survived the camp because he held to the reality that he was a doctor and therefore stayed with his patients despite any hope of escape or promises of release made by camp authorities.

In another part of his book, he described two men, each of whom had temporarily forgotten the meaning of their own lives in the pain of the moment. I confess there were many moments when I did the same. When you wish for your own extinction, you have forgotten what you know about the meaning of your own existence.

BEACH REFLECTION NO. 17

This old sailor loves to watch storm seas blast the shore from far off in the deep Pacific. He rests atop the first dune for safety as waves sweep powerfully onto the barrier of the dune. The ceaseless thunder and foaming whitecaps dressed overhead by a dark sky held him in equal parts of awe and fear. It was like the experience of life itself.

He did not know whether to hold or escape. At the moment, he could not say which was better. For now, he stayed.

HAIKU NO. 17

A haunting of surf
shivers through winter's chill air;
spray toasts the New Year.

CHAPTER 19

To Face a Sea of Troubles

I REACHED ONE OF MY most excruciating, irresolvable, and despair-ridden moments in 1980. With a dangerously low red blood cell count and no diagnosis, my college placed me on disability leave. I went into a hospital for a long stay. The moment was so awful because teaching had been taken away from me. I also had to leave my home and children for a place four hundred miles away. The situation was undefined. I naturally felt my life was coming to an end. In fact, I began to embrace the idea that my ill health would kill me. Why wouldn't it, when no one could explain what was wrong with me?

Day after day in the hospital I was sent for, tested,

and sent back to bed. There I would sit, blandly beige curtain around my bed in a room with four beds. A nurse would come, take my vital signs, and leave. They examined me from rump to ears, from toes to chin, and put me back to bed. I wandered the halls in a chintzy bathrobe and stupid elastic slippers. Television brought only irritation.

It seemed like a "finally" to me when, one day, within a curtain-enclosed bed, I began to talk to God. I told him that if this was the way things were going to be, he could take me right now. I meant it. Being fed up and sick of it, I just wanted him to end it and take me right then. I was more than ready as I sat in a kind of lotus position in the middle of the bed and bent my will to death.

Nothing happened, really, unless what happened next was my answer.

Perhaps an hour of demanding a solution from God passed. Then a nurse pulled back the curtains and told me it was time for a massage. Now that felt really good. It was the best kind of "laying on of hands."

The next day got better, when that same nurse brought me a guitar to play. I have no idea how she knew that I played guitar. She had borrowed it from her brother. Now I began to have a way of passing good time.

With a clearer head, I reasoned that she had known exactly what I had been feeling. She chose to help by bringing me a guitar, not by psychoanalyzing me or recommending drugs. It was her humane touch that changed my awful present into an endurable one. Stepping out of professional reserve and offering a discrete personal act is my idea of being saintly.

CHAPTER 20

A Comment on Suicide

IT'S WORTH REPEATING THE ADAGE that we often seek a permanent solution to a temporary problem. That adage often is used to describe suicide as a solution to personal problems. The idea is that even the most desperate situations are temporary. They pass. Nothing lasts–neither intense love nor hate, neither bankruptcy nor a good income, neither a broken heart nor broken water pipes. An unemployed person can find something else worth doing; a divorced person can find refuge with friends or another partner; or a convict can earn degrees, become religious, or take advantage of any self-development programs available. And a person who has gone blind can read

Braille or use talking books. All conditions in which we feel stuck have some more or less positive way out of them. We just need to let ourselves find them.

We are charged to live in the present moment. But what if the present moment is excruciating? Many of them are. No one ever told us we would run into irresolvable problems during our lives. Also, no one told us to drop any irresolvable problems and go do something else.

The thing about living in the present is that a new present shows up the next moment. We can cling to a crisis and suffer, or consider what is best for us and then take a new path. To remain in an excruciating, irresolvable, despair-ridden situation is to wish for a permanent solution to a temporary problem. Problems only last as long as we let them.

One signal bit of advice I learned from my daughter when she was sixteen. One day I asked her to wash the dishes. She said, "Whatever." Now, as her father, I felt the word as a dismissal. Yet it was not serious enough to warrant any action. I thought about it. The next time I asked her to wash the dishes, she again said, "Whatever." So I just said "whatever" back to her. It really irritated her, and the dismissal became a joke between us. Now I always suggest to people who don't like something that doesn't warrant any action just to say, "Whatever." It gets the point across and releases tension.

However, it takes more energy and more determination to dismiss big problems such as divorce, job loss, or a disabling condition. That is when it is most important to remember that the problem, as is the present moment, is temporary.

Eventually, doctors diagnosed my condition as Crohn's disease, and the cause was blood leaking through my intestines. Their treatments stopped it, and my red blood cell count began to return to normal.

Neither the diagnosis nor the treatment and neither returning home nor eventually returning to the classroom made things all better, but they were changed. Change is what is important when we feel we have reached a "dead" end. The reality of taking the first step toward change is that change is a process. It takes whatever time it takes. The main requirement is to hang on and let it come all the way into reality. If the wait seems hard, just try to imagine if it would have been better to hang on to excruciating and irresolvable pain.

What we know today is not what we will know tomorrow. What we feel now probably will not be what we feel later. My experience is that bad times always pass if one just steps away onto another path. To take the step may be difficult, but, if it is the right step, always succeeds. The same is true for what we think we know. Current knowledge just awaits contradiction and invites revision, as does a basket of apples sitting by the cider press. The apples can sit and rot or move on to be eaten or pressed into sweet cider. If we choose change, rather than immobility, new situations and new knowledge will move in. This we know.

BEACH REFLECTION NO. 18

It was a happy time when his daughter and her family came to visit. The grandchildren raised sand castles for hours on the beach. They flew kites and rode bicycles on the dune-top pathway. The most unusual experience for both grandchildren came from crabbing in the marina.

We all walked down onto the floats in the marina carrying the hoop and net. We attached a frozen chicken leg to the center of the hoop and net and dropped it twenty feet to the bottom of the bay.

After twenty minutes, we pulled the hoop up and found a scramble of crabs wrestling each other to get at the chicken.

The little girl, only four, began to squeal and back away from the wriggling mass.

Most of the crab were dropped back as too small, but two were placed in the bucket. As the day passed, the little girl grew comfortable with the ugly creatures and began oohing and ahhing over each catch.

By evening, a fresh crab feed was enjoyed by all, even the little girl.

HAIKU NO. 18

Crab boats tied to docks,
busily empty their holds.
Sea lions laze on floats.

CHAPTER 21

Keeping One's Mind in the Present: What a Bear Does in the Woods

DAD SAID OURS WAS A second-growth forest, but it felt primeval to a boy. Echoes of woodpeckers hammered through the woods as an aromatic summer shower passed. Each drop left dimples in the raw side of the logging road cut near our cabin. Several drops hung like dew on the orangish-red and black-dotted blossoms of tiger lilies sprouting by the roadside. Behind our cabin sweet ferns hung over a small spring. Some four gallons of water swelled in its basin and trickled over its verge to send a rivulet across the needled forest floor to disappear somewhere in the summer dust.

This was my home during the several summers Dad worked as an independent logger in the north Idaho woods. My uncle Hap and he dropped tamarack, Douglas fir, and cedars among huckleberry bushes and sweet ferns. There they lopped off branches and skimmed off the bark before sweating over the crosscut saw to fashion them into posts and poles. These they sold to lumber companies.

My brother Jack labored with them when he had to. I think it was because he was sixteen that Dad had to make so much noise to get him up in the morning. Once awake, I lay bathed in the shadows cast by kerosene lamps, warm under heavy quilts and smelling the pancakes, bacon, and eggs of the lumberjack breakfast they ate. I listened as they thumped from the cabin in their corked boots.

When I joined them later, my job was to gather the thick bark of the cedars and overlap their long, fuzzy, and richly scented slabs to make a roof and walls that sheltered me from periodic rain showers. Sometimes I could hear my uncle Hap raging as he horsed on a peavey to turn a bullheaded log, but somehow the innocence of the forest sheltered me from his cursing. I remember none of his words.

It's odd to me now that I was both alone and with my family in the forest. At eight years old, life in the forest entered me through visions of leaves, wind, and sunlight sending bars of gold down through the forest canopy. It was experience without judgment–all odors of bark, fern, and dust motes floating among massive trees. Sharp calls of "timber!" rang as a massive white pine thundered to drown the relentless swish of wind above me in the forest canopy.

Life was transparent, a complacency of childhood. Nowhere did I recognize good or bad, mean or nice; rain and dust came as they were.

Once in a while I would try for a sense of the now as it came out of the past. But I didn't grasp "second-growth forest" as anything but the forest of now. It was as it was to me, a rich tapestry of vision, sound, and smell, a feel of bark or blisters and the taste of morning pancakes covered in maple syrup. Being there was all there was, and it was more than enough.

Then my brother and I ran into the bear.

In all that I can recall, that was the first moment I became aware of meaning as applying to existence.

Life seeps into a child as raw information, accumulative but not interpreted. But until that summer, Dad and Mom meant only what they said and did. I saw life with them as actions and gestures, not of positive or negative conclusions.

Similarly, until that summer, love for my brother

lay implicit in his telling me ghost and monster stories in our dark bedroom, or inventing games with spent shotgun shells or crayon markings across the linoleum. He it was taught me to read time or dig carrots from frozen ground. Being angry at his ordering me around was an event, not a judgment.

Perhaps it was a Sunday with no other activity laid on us that he and I went exploring down the logging road. Perhaps we searched for wild raspberry or huckleberry to pick and eat. At times we were sent out with old coffee cans with wire handles to pick berries and return home with them. I don't recall if this was one of those times.

We strolled back along the worn road just taking in the heat, the dusty bushes, and the ferns when we came around a bend to confront a large brown bear.

Of course, we knew animals were in the forest. We practically lived with chipmunks and squirrels, sighted raccoon and woodchucks, porcupine and deer. Uncle Hap had shot a buck and hung it in the horse shed. But we had never spotted a bear. In fact, we had often been told that bears were shy of humans and were only rarely seen.

Jack and I stood frozen, the bear facing us only twenty yards down the road. He (I suppose because there was no cub) stood still to watch us.

Suddenly, Jack sprang away and disappeared into the trees with his loose jacket flapping behind him. The bear and I looked at each other for a long moment. Then he turned and walked with a rolling gait into the bushes on the other side of the road and also disappeared. I remember being struck by how his fur moved all over him as if it were trying to slip off.

The last to decide anything, I finally moved after my brother to go home.

While frozen, I had no thought of fear, no expectation, no reaction. But I was thoughtful as I walked. I realized that my brother had run off and left me alone to stand with the bear. I don't recall he even shouted for me to run. I connected that with the time when I was five years old. We had been crossing a street in Odessa when he started to run, stopped, and when I kept running had shouted for me to stop. Unfortunately, people were confusing me by shouting orders from both sides of the street. That made me pause long enough to be run over by a car. The vision of an undercarriage of frame and pipe passing over me remains in my head just as the scars do to this day.

This time, he kept running, and I remained.

All that thoughtfulness exposed something in my brother, for I had not known until then that I had learned to think a brother's job was to protect a brother. Yet my brother had run away and left me. This was like an epiphany, to go beyond experience to an understanding. I don't believe it had ever come to me that way before. I still did not think of the event in terms of good or bad, and I wish I had never learned to think of things that way. No, he was my brother, but now marked with a limitation, or just a specific sort of small, identifying mark. A check mark, maybe, not a flaw. Just something to remember in case it should ever be relevant again.

Years later, I learned the rest of the story about that day I got run over. I remember lying under a blanket near the old post office. How did I come to be a block away from where I'd been hit? Why couldn't I move? In time, I asked a man near me, "Why can't I move?" "You have a broken leg." There was no pain, but like a boy to an adult, I accepted the answer. It seemed I lay there a long time, while adults around me discussed failed attempts to get the only doctor to come down to help. He didn't come. Neither did my parents come. It was years before I learned that Jack had run the eight blocks home. Apparently, though, he loitered and hung around because he just couldn't tell my parents the bad news. A neighbor finally passed the word. Still, even when they arrived, darkness fell before I was placed in the car's backseat for the hour drive to the big city of Spokane. Then the pain began.

I remain glad that years passed before I learned Jack's part of the story. Meeting the bear gave me enough understanding for a child to carry.

What a bear does in the woods is pretty much what I did in the woods: to exist in the forest is to smell, taste, feel, hear, and see the multitude of trees and underbrush, the swarming life, like being drenched in surround sound, not just virtually, but physically. My eighth summer brought me from existence to the beginnings of meaning. Yet I am clear now that it was existence that taught me meaning. Now I try always not to impress meaning on existence. Moment to moment events test my knowledge. My knowledge does not define each new event.

We can only grope at what a bear knows, in the way I knew something about my brother. Perhaps we use our own experience of existence to grasp what a bear does in the woods. As the joke goes, the bear lives free to come and go anywhere he wants. He is free to be, to think or not, to stare and turn from an intruding boy and wander off perhaps to the same berry patch, perhaps to mate or to sleep. We don't tell the bear what to believe or what to do. Probably we understand something of the irrelevance of our value systems to the bear or, for that matter, to any of the other animals that abide on the earth with us.

There is a seductiveness to the idea we should live as unconsciously as we think animals do, simply and in harmony with the all. As we are not identical with other animals, neither can we or should we live like them. As they all live according to their own natures, so must it be for us. Yet, in common with them, humans enter existence empty of beliefs, judgments, or values. We have a certain form, specific yet wide-ranging inherited traits, but we are empty of conclusions. These, our families, our surrounding culture, and our personal experiences imprint on us as we grow. In particular among animals, we are free to examine earlier imprinting, change what we wish, and live by our own understandings.

Sometimes we may find it difficult to compensate for damage inflicted in the past, but like a bear, we remain free to make of life whatever we want. It's up to us to discover the how. In short, we are born with the freedom; what remains is to find the determination and allow ourselves to find our own paths.

What a boy learned during those summers in the woods is that even we humans can live as free to exist in our own way as that brown bear.

BEACH REFLECTION NO. 19

Usually he dressed warmly for the beach's chilly conditions, so he felt surprise to meet a thirty-something woman in a bikini by the water's edge. It seemed odd to have her face him directly and ask so seriously what he felt about the City Council allowing so many homes to be built on the first dune.

He admitted that he had asked the mayor to stop building on the dune but had gotten only a "hmm" in answer.

Soon, she turned and walked back up to her house on the first dune. He settled among a scattering of stones to wonder when storm and tide would overwhelm the dune and rush into those homes. The sea always won against the shore.

HAIKU NO. 19

The house sits too near
the shore of washaway beach,
lives built on wet sand.

CHAPTER 22

The Child Is Father of the Man

THE SEEDS OF WHO YOU are lie in your childhood. That is because the generative power of childhood taps deep roots and extends long years toward multiple generations. To look at a baby during his first few months is to see only undirected movements and animal urges such as hunger or discomfort. In him, however, lies the basic characteristics of the man or woman that baby develops into during the longest developmental period in the animal world. We know some of us are born more shy, others more outgoing, but it takes time to begin to grasp a picture of the person to be. Yet the basic stuff is there, molded, modified. or even misdirected, but still there to be dealt with throughout life.

We parents who fill whole rooms with toys and distract children with the electronic rattles of television quite mistake the vast potentials growing up among us. Who can doubt that the degree to which we have little time to give our children runs equivalent to the trappings we lay about them? We parents can love them and hold them with affection, or neglect them and send them off to distractions, but what these influences do to children is either to make it easier or more difficult for them to realize their own positive potentials.

Wordsworth may be pardoned for saying in another poem that children come into this life "trailing clouds of glory." Why not repeat it and understand it. Children constitute an opportunity to influence the next generation. Will we parents do it well, or botch the chance? That is the only power we have, except the personal power to make the best of our own lives. What have we gained as adults if we lose the youthful sense of wonder? Wonder it is that keeps us open to lifelong learning. That is why I say we should never lose sight of who we were as children.

The old seventies lore of transactional analysis remains relevant today. Indeed, as we grow and develop, we retain much of the child we were as we learn first to be the adult and then the parent. However, as each of us contains a unique individual, we may ask how to self-discover what elements of self we have brought forward into our adult and parental selves. Basic characteristics may evolve or moderate but remain basic, we hear. Any parent knows that no two children are alike, so it is obvious certain basic traits energize them from the start. These may be more difficult to identify years later in the suit-wearing, smooth-talking businessman or the quiet gardener trimming the grass, but probably the essentials remain active.

I argue that knowing our own essentials gives us the best chance to begin knowing who we are, our inmost selves, the people many of us try to hide from others. Once we realistically grasp our own natures, we can begin to live more effectively. We must let ourselves see the truth.

We all have heard someone say, "Wake up and smell the roses." Many of us don't even realize we fell asleep. Someone has to give us the wake-up call. Our culture comes filled with exhortations to keep our minds in the present. Few of us, however, would say, "Let me die," if we lost our sense of wonder somewhere along the way. I would rather say that to lose our sense of the moment is a kind of death.

My boyhood gave me the touchstones I needed to remind me what it feels like to live in the present. For one thing, being present means doing, not waiting to do or thinking about doing. My father gave me my first bicycle when I entered elementary school. It gave me more pleasure than any number of talking alphabet toys or Thomas the Train videos. My Wards Thorndike bike played as my freedom, my speed to the hill, and my motorcycle by clipping two playing cards to the rear spokes. It also crashed me and rode me away from threats. My mother used to say that she always knew where I was. My only answer to that was, "You'll always know where I am; I'm out!" Try that with a TV.

My bicycle taught me that freedom was the essence of childhood, as I have learned it is the essence of being a man. Beyond that, a child has an immediacy to his days that we intellectuals call "being present." So many philosophies urge us to be present that it really lies past doubt.

Much of my youth was spent out in nature. Father took me to lakes enclosed by volcanic cliffs to hunt ducks, to serene forested lakes for fishing, and to ocean shores for camping. Those places have left indelible marks on my character. Most of what I think and feel is connected to nature. This book most clearly celebrates my love of the sea and its shores.

Some would say, "So what?" Some would also say the sense of wonder about nature's beauties has little to do with self-knowledge. But it does. The sense of wonder opens us to seeing ourselves in the world around us. It prompts being present in the moment, smelling the roses, tasting the wine, and acknowledging the gift of affection from loved ones and friends. The first trick is to see. Our sense of wonder, can we sustain it throughout life, keeps us seeing. The second part is to work at understanding what we see. Basic to all this is to allow ourselves to think for ourselves rather than adhere to any of the many dogmas our experiences seem to try to force on us. We must try to cling to self-determination and an ongoing process of checking our perceptions.

BEACH REFLECTION NO. 20

In many a January the beachcomber's brother came to sit beside him on the beach. Side by side in their canvas chairs, they would pass a bottle of Cabernet Sauvignon back and forth. And, of course, they would talk.

The beachcomber couldn't wait to tell his dog story. To him it illustrated how persistently we believe what we want to. Believe. This is the story he told:

"One day my next-door neighbor said to me, 'Your dog pooped on my lawn. Please keep him in your yard.'

"I asked him to show me the place. He walked over and pointed down. There lay two rather small droppings.

"I said, 'These are from a small dog. Mine is a big dog. Besides, you must have seen that I keep him on a leash and pick up after him. It must be some other dog.'

"He walked back to his car. He opened his car door to get in and then called over to me, 'Dogs don't poop in my yard.'"

My brother laughed. "Dogs poop anywhere they want to," he said, "I think they actually go out of their way to outrage us."

The beachcomber told his brother that he had driven back a few days later and saw his neighbor's beagle pooping right where those other droppings had been. Apparently he believed his dog didn't poop.

The brothers chuckled together and passed the bottle, again.

"I have one too," his brother said. As usual, he had been staring out at a distant fishing boat passing far out to sea.

"I've seen the same thing many times with some

parents. They simply cannot see that their little darlings have or ever could do anything wrong. An acquaintance of mine never believed that her ten-year-old son had stolen her roommate's Folger's can full of coins amounting to some fifty dollars. In the face of that denial, the roommate eventually moved out. The child eventually offered a partial confession, but as far as I know, my acquaintance never reimbursed her former roommate."

The beachcomber asked, "What happened then?"

"During the following years, she always seemed surprised when he committed another theft."

Neither brother could figure out what possible benefit it would be to them to hold on to their unrealistic attitudes toward the dog and the boy. Neither position bears any value for making life better.

The brothers finally emptied the bottle, laid it in the sand, and let the noisy silence of the ocean take hold of them. At least they could hope that the next beach walker with a dog on a leash would stop long enough to reach down to pick up its droppings.

HAIKU NO. 20

He runs beside logs
catching his lead on branch stubs
whiffing adventure.

CHAPTER 23

Disability as a Moving Target

NO TWO PEOPLE GO BLIND or experience blindness in the same way. I became blind step by step over a period of thirty years. Each successive step shocked me immobile. It angered me to face another task I was able to do the day before but not this morning. Back I would go to the ophthalmologist for more eye drops. No matter what, the drop in vision remained. Gradually I adapted to a new and lesser equilibrium.

To put it bluntly, my type of vision loss made me go through crisis after crisis and year after year. Along the way I learned a lot about coping with crisis. Some coping comes easily, some only later, or from an outside source. Every time I had to rethink what life meant to me. We hear constantly that self-knowledge comes in a flash. No. These flashes arrive every time we enter a new crisis point. In my case, they came between six months to two years after I turned twenty-five. Some few I ignored and soldiered on. More took me to the mat, where I saw I needed to do things differently.

While my right ankle froze dramatically during a basketball game, most disabilities or crises don't generally strike so hard. Both divorces and my loss of eyesight crept on me in slow stages, at first nearly imperceptibly.

In the world of eyes, to be blind means to have lost the ability to do some of life's normal activities. In the world of eyes, to be blind does not mean "stone blind" or completely without vision. A person begins being blind when they cannot read print even with corrective lenses. The simplest definition is a visual acuity of 20/200. Once beyond that point, you are visually impaired or, for all practical purposes, blind. Blindness, in common with other disabilities, makes some or most of life's normal activities either difficult or impossible. In fact, when a person cannot do one or more of life's normal activities, that defines disability in the Americans with Disabilities Act of 1990. Back in the early days of personal computers, I found I could see an amber screen better than black and white. Using that, I began work on a novel. One morning when I went to my computer, I could no longer read even the amber screen. The drop in vision often happened just like that. So I added screen magnification software. Then came another sudden loss, and only a speech synthesizer would do. Using key commands, I could listen to what I wrote or read all messages and commands.

Once I could operate a computer entirely with speech, successive losses of vision didn't require any further enhancements. However, these computer applications forced a continuous and steep learning curve over the course of a dozen years. As fast as technology changes, so must I, or give up.

The first symptom that my eyesight was going wrong was a sensitivity to light so severe that one day I drove home from work wearing three pairs of sunglasses. Luckily, three of them were in the glove box. Without them, I would have never made it home because without them I couldn't have kept my eyes open. It turned out that this condition was called "iritis."

My opthalmologist could not explain why these eye inflammations happened or why they persisted against his strongest treatment. He would call my arthritis doctor to consult, and I remember him saying once, to my arthritis doctor, "You could make me look good if you could figure this out." I think now he suspected I had an underlying autoimmune disease. That turned out some years later to be Crohn's disease.

I moved, and the new ophthalmologist saw that my optic nerve was looking pale and that it was "cupping." He didn't know why cupping should occur. The pressure in my eyes measured between eighteen and twenty-eight, and damage to my optic nerve shouldn't be happening. So much for the uselessness of the word "should." So now we use the term, "Don't 'should' on yourself."

During that same period, cataracts clouded my left eye, so he removed a cataract in my left eye. When he took off the bandage, I had no central vision in my left eye. All he said when he found I had gone blind in that eye was, "Hmm." I had a much stronger reaction.

Had he advised me to seek help for my blindness, I surely would have had the will to do so. But at that point I did not have the well of information, ways of dealing with the crisis, or the wisdom to clearly see how desperate was my need. All was confusion and pain. I am not sure I even discussed it with my first wife. My doctor, after all, said only, "Hmm."

Blindness does have serious consequences for some relationships. I know that it contributed to my two divorces. It isn't easy for loved ones to watch a person go blind; it also isn't easy for the one going blind to notice how his terror affects his partners. I can illustrate that impact by relating words said to me by my second wife, even after seventeen years since the divorce. She said to me, "I had eight hard years of marriage with you." Still, marriage to her and all that happened during that period wasn't a picnic for me, either.

My first wife agreed to drive me the two hundred miles to the vision specialists in Albuquerque, New Mexico. All day the doctors tested my visual field and eye pressure, and examined the back of my eye with eye drops meant to expand or contract my iris. By the end of the day, my eyes had been strained almost beyond endurance. They diagnosed "low-pressure glaucoma." Now, glaucoma is a condition characterized by high pressure in the eye. So what was "low-pressure" glaucoma? In other words, at the eye pressure that damaged my optic nerve, most doctors would not have been concerned. In my case, those pressures did damage my optic nerve, and I continued to lose vision.

As my wife drove me the two hundred miles

back home, she told me she was ready to divorce me. Sore tears hurt my already sore eyes. Now wasn't that a fine end to a bad day? Like this moment in the car, life does not allow us to cope with one crisis at a time. I was unready to deal with two dirty tricks at once: low-pressure glaucoma, itself an oxymoron, and being asked for a divorce moments after getting the diagnosis. Within five years I was in my second marriage and had reached the visual acuity called "legally blind."

What we call blindness lies in the continuum between "legal" blindness (20/200 to totally blind. Only 15 percent of blind people are totally blind. Blindness refers to the whole of that continuum because such a condition means you cannot read print, even with corrective lenses. One stage of vision decline came on me one morning as I sat again at my amber monitor to continue work on the book I was writing. But this morning I could not read the amber screen. It took awhile to absorb the shock. Soon, though, I embarked on an even more ambitious accommodation: I wrote a grant and got support from Colorado Rehabilitation Services and the college to purchase a computer, scanner, printer, and speech and magnification software. I changed assignments in my writing courses to have papers handed in to me on floppy disks instead of typed or handwritten papers. For a time I based class presentations on notes I wrote in black markers on yellow notepads. Vision dropped again, so I taped notes on a recorder and listened to them during class using an earplug.

None of these losses of vision were easy to endure, but the worst came in 2001 when suddenly liquid flowed down my face like some kind of a gusher. It didn't pour from my nose or mouth, and when I realized the origin was my right eye, I got as hysterical as I've ever been in all my life. After a 911 call and subsequent calls for advice, I found an ophthalmologist who would take me for a consultation. Doctor McKillop studied my eye with an intensity I'd not experienced for many years. He said that a corneal lesion had opened, and all the aquatic body had drained from my eye. After lengthy reflection, he advised me that while he could reconstruct my eye, it would never look right again. He followed that by saying, further, that because my eye had suffered a trauma, it was imperative to have the eye removed. He said it had been known since the Civil War that a trauma to one eye was followed all too often by a similar consequence in the other eye. Soon a surgeon removed my eye and surgically imbedded a ball inside the interior tissue. After my surgery healed, Erickson

Laboratories created an acrylic prosthetic eye whose appearance exactly duplicated the appearance of my remaining eye.

I am now used to wearing a "false" eye, but I promise the operation and recovery period strained me as much as the amputation of a limb would have.

First, I hated going into public with a hollow socket. Many of those I knew commiserated by saying, "Well, you had no vision in that eye anyway, did you?" Some people might have answered, "Well, my nose doesn't see either, but I still wouldn't like to have it removed." The loss of my right eye seemed quite drastic enough to me. Why is it that we expect people to understand what they have not experienced? It is difficult but sometimes best if people put aside the guide of their own experience and simply take the word of someone who knows.

My remaining eyesight continues to decline as I write. I know that at some point in the future I will have no vision at all. One thing you surely gain over the years is the confidence that you know how to cope.

BEACH REFLECTION NO. 21

It is the rare beachcomber who doesn't bring a dog along. In this man's case, he always brought along his guide dog, Commodore. Commodore would rush around all the logs and sticks he could reach on the twenty-five-foot flexi-lead. Other times he liked running through shallow water in the ebb tide. Then he would race in large circles, throwing sand up behind his haunches.

One day after such a sprint, the man paused long enough to reflect. He realized that during all his time on the beach, he had never found an agate. Friends told him they spotted agate by their special gleam from the sand. He had not caught such a gleam yet, and probably wouldn't.

In a sweep of grief for his lost eyesight, he whispered a prayer. "Please, God, grant me an agate." Pressure under his left shoe caught his attention. He bent to pick it up. In great surprise, he rolled a large agate through his fingers.

HAIKU NO. 21

In chill tide's backwash
a host of sanderlings hop
to snatch crustaceans.

CHAPTER 24

Joy in Life despite Diminishing Returns

SO THERE I WAS, IN the late eighties, getting around using a white cane, pretty lame, and with painful hands, low red blood cell count, and once divorced, already. I still had fun. I owned and rode a quarter horse named El Caliente, traveled all over Colorado, New Mexico, and Arizona, enjoyed community concerts and art galleries, as well as my children's sports. Of course, I still taught college full time and acted in community theater productions. All these continued despite three disabling conditions.

None of this means life was rosy. In any bouquet of roses, in time petals will begin to drop. Blindness was beginning to damage my status at college. Since that has to do with job loss, I'll take up the problem later. More rose petals dropped from relations with my second wife. Since divorce comes up in more detail, later, for now it is enough to say that we soon got divorced. Relations had begun to sour, partly due to my stepson's destructive behavior and partly due to how differently we each saw life. As a result of declines such as these, by the early nineties, I had left college teaching for a disability management position and had begun an extramarital affair. Of course, so did my second wife. All the errors I had committed helped me decide to leave my disability management position and move out of state. Sometimes, we hope not often, the best path is just to leave.

Does a person continue to find enjoyment in life when he seems to lose his familiar pleasures?

When a person goes through grief and loss there always comes a time when it is difficult to feel that there will ever be any happiness again.

One time I was telling Mary, a friend of mine, that I was going to live in France for a year. She looked very puzzled at my excitement. She asked, "Why do you want to go to France?" I asked her what she meant. "Well, you can't see anything there," she said. I told her that maybe she had forgotten the good wine and excellent food of France, not to mention the interesting culture.

In hearing my own words, I realized that no matter how diminished my eyesight, I continued to take pleasure in what I could still see and experience. The enjoyment of life is not dependent on the amount of vision a person retains. The same is true for deafness, weakness, pain, or any other disabling condition. There is much left even after a person can no longer drive a car.

Continued love of life derives from recognizing the pleasures still to be experienced. The thing is to trust in the timeline our consciousness travels along whereby we know where we have been and know we are still moving forward along that line. Yes, Virginia, there really is a future. We all know that while we go through grief and loss, the goal is to achieve acceptance of our limitations. We would like acceptance to be a simple matter of exclaiming, "Oh, rapture, I have accepted my disability!" Acceptance is more complicated than that. Yet acceptance is the line at which we can once again begin to enjoy life. That is also the point at which we may be able to offer what we've learned to others.

In my experience, there are two types of acceptance: giving up and going on. In 1988 I failed the eyesight test during my driver's license exam. Even though it was no surprise, the event created a great emptiness within me. Luckily, soon after, I met Jerry Kuns, who came to help me adjust to my encroaching blindness. Jerry was already well known among blind people, especially for running a personal business in San Francisco conducting tours of the city under the name "Jose Can You See Tours. We who suffer disabilities are often tempted to fade into the background of our own lives. We might feel like giving up friends, work, or even our pleasures. I, too, have been tempted to give up, but I could never see any fun in it.

The temptation to fade out always returns unless a person learns to manage the disability. It isn't enough to say, "I'm fine, now." If I can't drive a car, I have to learn to take public transportation or ask people for rides. To succeed in using new methods, I must learn the skills involved, such as where to get bus rider information or procure and maintain disability passes. If we are excessively independent minded, we need to learn to ask for help, to combine our efforts with others to make our environments more supportive and accessible.

To accept the ways in which we become diminished requires new skills, positive attitudes, and a continuous search for better methods of doing things. At any point, had I given up and faded out, I would not have met Jerry Kuns or joined the National Federation of the Blind (NFB). That organization provided me with a philosophy of blindness and a focus on helping to remove social barriers. Without what I learned from the NFB, I might not have been open to learning how to cope from friends, organizations, and rehabilitation professionals. By giving up, I would not have gone to an extensive blindness skills training program or worked hard to gain skill in using adaptive equipment with computers.

Facing disability has also taught me the value of embracing an existential self. By being committed to life and lifelong learning, by concentrating on being present in all situations, I have survived losses that could have stunned me into immobility. By refusing the dependency offered by friends and society in general to blind and disabled persons, I lived how I needed to live, not how those with little understanding of blindness may have wished me to live.

HAIKU NO. 22

Moonlight fills the room
hanging in a deep blue sky
one more sleepless night.

PART 5

Relationships:
The Real Rocket Science

BEACH REFLECTION NO. 22

Often when the beachcomber returned home, he sat right down to write a haiku that reflected his meditations. One of those follows this reflection. Yes, on that day, the flights of birds reminded him of how many times he acted as instinctively as any animal to all but the last woman he took up with.

At twenty-two, he came out of the navy and proposed to the first woman he could talk to. There was never much else to their life together.

His second marriage and first girlfriend after that were purely sexual adventures. No rationality was involved, no assessment of compatibility, and sheer denial of obvious character flaws that he couldn't endure for long. His next girlfriend after that shone with a good and cheerful nature but was incapable of entering into a shared life.

Did those gulls flying by do better with their mating? He had every reason to think that most of them did. He knew, now, what he had done wrong in all those cases. He also knew it would have been much better to have seen the issues more clearly before he got involved with those five women, all with good sides and worse sides, while he was driven either by his illusions or his passion.

Always he had wanted to mate for life, like the

geese just now flying overhead, honking out their chatty voices to each other.

HAIKU NO. 23

They laugh as their jeep swerves
at a flock of sanderlings.
wheels sinkwhile birds fly.

CHAPTER 25

The "Truth" and the Self: How to Go Wrong in Relationships

WHEN YOU LET YOURSELF SEE your truth, what is the "truth" you are seeing? The only word I can think of that is more slippery than the word "truth" is the word "love." Love I will come to later. The only kind of truth I care about in this book is the truth of who we individually are.

For example, at no time in my life did I ever ask myself what I needed in a relationship with a lover or spouse. Suddenly, my daughter bought me a gift membership in eHarmony, an online couples matching service. At its front end was an extensive psychological assessment of personal needs and attitudes. The first question asked what three things we most needed in a partner. Why couldn't I have learned years ago the three things I needed in a long-term relationship? First, I needed someone who both wanted and was capable of a long-term relationship. Second, I needed someone who was both self-reliant and deeply affectionate. Third, I needed someone who loved reading and was a good conversationalist. Had I worked out these answers earlier in life, perhaps I could have avoided two divorces and two dead-end affairs. The truth about myself came out in my eHarmony test. But we need to understand who we are much earlier in life.

We may come closer to knowing what makes us ourselves when we begin our questioning from the concept of personal authenticity. I use the word "truth" to say that we can only be in harmony with the world around us by being true to who we are. Basically, authenticity means not letting others run your life. At the same time, I grant that learning who we are is not easy. Many forces around us attempt to bend us this way and that way. Charting a course of personal honesty through such pressures has no sure outcome. However, the struggle is worth it as the only way to become our authentic selves.

There is no disputing that only the individual is

qualified to make decisions affecting his or her own life. Who else could have the personal insight, the self-understanding, to know what the best course of personal action is? Only three of us can guide our selves: me, myself, and I. Accept that, and we begin to live both more dangerously and more fully.

Not only do we need to choose life for ourselves, we have to grant that power to everyone else.

First off, you may want something for yourself that the other person does not want. Even worse, you may be wrong about yourself and may be mistaken about your desire. Desires work for us and against us. There is nothing more human than wanting something or someone we shouldn't want. Then, too, we purposely compromise ourselves to meet peer pressure or social directives.

An example of this kind of double error hit me when I asked a particular woman to marry me. The situation was as romantic as I could make it. The moment came in a beautiful old-style inn beside a scenic lake near Niagara Falls, just the way any romantic proposal should happen. Despite that, the woman refused to look at the ring I offered. She wouldn't acknowledge my proposal. Back in our room, she refused even to discuss my proposal. During the following months, she made it as much of a nonevent as possible. Refer back to my three basic needs, and it is easy to understand why we eventually broke up. First and foremost, my own sexual desire led me to make the proposal to a person who violated those basic needs I later and finally identified. In addition, I diverted my good sense in the socially determined romantic haven in which proposals are supposed to happen. I am still not sure what sort of "blindness" led me to believe she wanted my proposal. My women friends put it all more simply by saying I was led by a smaller part of my body than my brain.

We humans are not just bodies. At the highest philosophical level, we must think of our bodies also as a field in relation to the world we inhabit. Our universe is not defined simply in terms of physical bodies such as suns, planets, and the physical elements of them, but also of the magnetic, electrical, molecular, and quantum forces flowing in and among them. Such forces create fields that affect each other. Likewise, our selves consist as bodies interacting in an environment just as a magnetic field does in physics. Thus, we exist as part of all that exists. In my example, I needed to attend to my body's impulses as well as my possible rationality, but to my putative partner's actual identity too.

Many times I have mistaken my own motives as

well as misunderstood others. We are neither perfect, nor do we live in a perfect world. When we mistake ourselves or others, we can adjust our interpretations to reflect the reality we experienced. To let myself see my own truth depends on my desire to do so and my awareness that to become clear about one's own self involves a process, not a result.

To be on the trail of the human is to live in the present, believe in the right to choose life, beware of predictable errors of thought, and remember to grant these things to everyone else.

BEACH REFLECTION NO. 23

When he walked the path to the beach, all he felt and thought went with him. Burdened or carefree, depending on events, he unsnapped his canvas chair and pressed its legs firmly into the sand. Then he sat, looking out to sea. The action of waves, the push of wind, or the cries of birds might drag him from contentment into worry or worry into contentment. On a given day, the ebb and flow of emotion might settle into placidity. On the ebb tide, the sea itself would often lie down in a quiet sort of restlessness. Then the outer and inner worlds would correspond. That was best. Then he could think clearly and weightlessly.

He came to know that the sea returned him to himself–who and why he was. Such knowledge was hard to hold, so every day he blessed the sea.

HAIKU NO. 24

When surf flushes them,
the sanderlings rise like smoke
puffed aloft as one.

CHAPTER 26

The Wages of Denial

ONE DARK, SLIPPERY NIGHT I stood by the pylons of a footbridge across the River of Lost Souls. Familiarly called just the Animas River, it swelled above a bottleneck before swiftly flowing through the city of Durango, Colorado. The spring flood rose high and pushed past the footbridge with immense strength. It swelled darkly over the closest pylon.

My parents had taught me the blessings of a lifelong marriage. Never could I have imagined the despair that now gripped me in the desperate passions of divorce. None of my greatest efforts to touch my wife's emotions, not all of my professions of love or arguments about retaining our family had the least effect on my wife's determination to continue her affair.

So here I was, standing by the darkly rushing river wishing to drop into the deepest part. Surely that fate would kill my shame over losing my marriage.

How cold the river looked. The few lights that reflected on the water shivered into squiggly lines. Surely no sound of weeping or even scream of fear could reach the house lights perched on the heights above the Animas. What would it be like to be swept under? Much of this river rose in fourteen-thousand-foot mountains still holding massive snowfalls. How cold would the water be?

Suddenly I found myself laughing. How could I laugh under such a cloud of helplessness and failure? I laughed at my foolishness. You don't really want to die if you are worried about getting cold and wet. It calmed me to laugh, and soon I walked back up the hill to the conflict filling my home.

Sometimes you want to die when you feel caught in a trap. The trap exists because a person doesn't see that he has a right to decide what to do for himself. Simple, huh? I needed to let myself see my truth. I could choose to divorce her, not to wait for her to tell me what she wanted. I've met people who faced two broadly defined courses of action. Instead of choosing, they waited for one axe or the other to fall. In other words, they wanted to let outside forces decide the course of their lives. They hung up on their inability to choose what they, personally, wanted to do, how they wanted to live. A woman friend of mine saw a marriage counselor over a period of time. At lat, the counselor told her to come back next week with a decision as to whether or not to stay in her marriage. Forced to do so, she decided to stay and felt swamped with relief to have decided, despite knowing her counselor thought she would decide the other way.

A similar dilemma faced me more than once.

BEACH REFLECTION NO. 24

There came the day he associated watching the sea roll in with his time in the navy. Two years at sea between his sophomore and junior college years marked his life in a permanent way. In a very real manner, his now on the beach and then on the rolling breast of the Pacific Ocean made a full circle. So he wrote what follows.

POEM NO. 1: A WORN-OUT SAILOR

A worn-out sailor, he
no longer goes to sea.
He takes his canvas chair,
settles its legs in sand
near to where tide lands
to sit, secure, to stare
as every rippling wave
rows toward the shore
like boats oared by slaves.
He counts each by each
as they hit upon the beach
to see if it were true
that every seventh wave
would flow all the way to,
but not to wet, his feet.
A strange watch to keep,
his look so steady and grave,
nothing can shift his glance,
not the chance of passersby,
not the little birds that dance
on a beach littered with shells
or gulls swirling in the sky,
but just the magic of waves
and how memory held him in thrall.

He thrilled to new ports of call,
not old routines but new places,
and his buddies' friendly faces;
best was the palm-lined canal
to fabulous Pearl Harbor
where giant ships lay enshrined,
and he learned to drink and dine
in Polynesian bars.
Oh, Hong Kong's swarming sampans,
Manila's sweaty rains,
Kaoschiung's polluted port
where Lee "Lynne" Chou held court,
the tattoo he got in PI:
whatever was exotic he tried.

All his service held drama,
even such more quiet days,
as docking in a green bay
so clear to the rock-strewn bottom
that he might touch each reef.
On the most serene of days,
an ocean panorama
stretched from horizon to horizon,
vast as an earth-sized beast
breathing like a bellows in motion
around a scatter of keys.

Then came the sea that thundered,
whipped by massive typhoons,
to fill him with awestruck wonder
as the sea swelled so high
it hid any sight of sky.

Mind full of now and then,
faced with this shoreline reach,
what holds him in timeless when
on a lonely stretch of beach?
Perhaps it is the counted waves
that measure the remainder of his days.
Perhaps he is only tired
with the effort of being retired.
He leaves it to the ocean scene
to decipher what he means.
A worn-out sailor, he
no longer goes to sea.

HAIKU NO. 25

Like a homeless god
a fierce wind wracks our small home;
like fear, it passes.

CHAPTER 27

Accepting the Right to Choose

I AM PRO-CHOICE BECAUSE I cannot know enough about another person to choose for them. Being pro-choice is not to approve of abortion; the several women I know who have had abortions did so in critical circumstances, and have wept at the memory of their losses. Anti-abortionists tell a convenient lie when they say that women are casual about abortions. Only a person who never had one could consider it a casual thing to do.

Each of us must choose for ourselves, simply because no one else can possibly know what we are dealing with. Other people also do not have to live with the consequences of the decisions they may wish to force on us.

There is another way to illustrate the complexity of choice.

When I received my doctorate in English, my course work did not include a class on methods of teaching college. I had to figure it out for myself. After three years, my college at the time had a 25 percent drop in enrollment, and I was released. That gave me a great shock, or, as the saying goes, "a wake-up call." After four months of idleness, I was lucky to find part-time teaching at a nearby university. I decided to throw out everything I had done before and begin from scratch. I borrowed course descriptions from every experienced professor I could find and based my own course plans on them. Through extensive study of dissertations about teaching methods and reading teaching journals, I evolved these descriptions until they would not have been recognizable to my original sources. In short, I had finally developed an approach to teaching that worked for me but would not work for anyone else. I believe that college professors work from plans unique to themselves. They've all had to evolve personal styles in order to be effective. The same principle applies to choosing how to live an effective life.

BEACH REFLECTION NO. 25

Every day brought the beachcomber new sights. A small flock of eight brown pelicans roosted quietly by the seawall as he went into the Highlander restaurant. There work was done for the day. From an observation deck he saw a seal perched six feet up on a rocking channel buoy. He wondered how it could have gotten so high. When he bought a fresh salmon from a fishing boat, the fisherman filleted it and tossed the spine to a sea lion lounging in the water off the stern. It gulped noisily, and the meal slipped down smoothly. No chewing was required. The sea lion huffed and rolled lazily while he waited for the next handout.

"You wouldn't see things like that in a city," he told himself comfortably. He loved the sea-its life, its immense power, its ability to bring peace to his soul. He lived in anticipation of the next wave, next sand dollar, next bikinied woman. All of it was important.

HAIKU NO. 26

In the warm, wet fall
clouds of mosquitoes greet us.
We pray for fall winds.

CHAPTER 28

Divorce No. 1: Fear of Flying

DIVORCE IS ONLY THE CONCLUSION of a process of dissolution. The actual divorce gives enough pain, but the process leading to it runs us through many pains, frequent doubts, and terrified strokes of fear for what will become of us. Our weaknesses will rise and direct us if they can; our strengths will seem irrelevant. Those who deal well with the dissolution of a marriage have a right to some pride over that, but my only pride, and it is not much, is that I never called my wife names nor became violent. Otherwise, I made every mistake possible.

One of the hardest challenges I ever faced was to let myself see that my first wife was beginning a love affair. I saw the signs. I felt the fear. At one cocktail party the man followed her around as if he were her puppy. After everyone left, I complained about that. She just said, "I'll take care of it." And I let her get away with that dismissal. That was to establish my pattern of nonaction for the next three years: avoidance, denial, ducking, jigging aside, hoping, ignoring, suffering silently. You name it, I did it.

As I will describe later, I finally did have to face the truth. It was just so hard to face what I knew would be a very hard thing to get through. I didn't want to go through it, so I didn't let myself see it for a long time.

Here's what I endured: the surprise imposition of her lover's company as we dined out, his sitting on her other side when we attended our children's games, keeping silence when I found he had given her flowers on her birthday when I delivered mine. Then, of course, she lied when she told me in front of her classroom full of students that they had given her the flowers.

In other words, I wouldn't have felt the need to delude myself had I revealed that I caught the flagrant lie. I did not.

Our very existence makes us free to choose the course of our own lives. To accept this is to begin the realizations that smoothes the way to personal clarity and accurate decision making. This clarity of perception is what I call truth. Truth is not an absolute, but, like everything else in personal experience, is a matter of constant growth and development. What we need to find is a way to let our minds range through a number of ways of seeing any situation we encounter. What a temptation it is to freeze into one posture in any situation. If we could find a way to keep our minds free to think, to consider, and not to yield to habitual patterns of thought, we would have found a way to "let" ourselves "see" the "truth."

From the first moment I suspected my first wife was becoming involved with one of her colleagues, I felt helpless, distraught, and confused. I couldn't understand why she often went to bars after work instead of coming home. She said she met there with coworkers; she came home smelling of smoke, but explained that the bar was smoke-filled. One time I rode with her in her car. When she stopped, a pack of cigarettes and a lighter slid from under the passenger seat. "Oh," she said, "those must be G---'s." What was he doing in her car? Since I learned later that she smoked, which I never knew, she expressed only one of the many lies she told and which I saw but swallowed.

Worse was to come, and I had to swallow incredibly obvious betrayals. She worked evenings at a local motel restaurant. One night I drove down to visit, and there sat her colleague. What could have been more obvious? Yet I didn't act. That is obvious: I hoped she would end her affair voluntarily.

Then came the day when her colleague's wife called to tell me she had kicked him out of her house for having an affair with my wife. When she came home that evening, I finally had to confront her. I made her sit down. I said, "Are you having an affair?" As if I didn't know. She turned her head away and said, "I don't even know what an affair is." Imagine what I said to clarify that. She didn't respond, so I asked, "Have you had sex with him?" She said, "Just once." Now I turn my face away at the enormity of the lie. My heart sank, for no matter how much I had suppressed my grasp of the situation, I knew, deeply and truly, that to begin with a lie was to doom our relationship. At that point, I knew I should tell her to pack her bag and go to join her lover in his own exile. After all, that had been her choice. What held me, still, was the wish, unrealistic as it was, that she would end the affair at some time and come back to me and our children.

She never did. Now that the affair was

acknowledged, she came home at midnight in his car. Met him daily for lunches and even some of our dinners out. Joined us at our children's games and let even her other colleagues and the public witness her now public scandal.

What did I do? I agonized. I shouted at her, begged her to stop. Twice had her lie that she had stopped. Caught her on the phone with him in our house. I constantly asked, "Why is she doing this to me?"

I wondered later how a person with my education and life experience could have continued to ask the wrong question for so long. I kept wishing for her to fix the problem. I did not remember to take responsibility for my own life. I had been leaving it in her hands. That ended the weekend I totaled our car when a drunk in a pickup crept across the highway right in front of my daughter and I. As I waited in the hospital to learn if my daughter's jaw was broken or just injured, I called my wife to let her know what happened. "Thanks for letting me know," she said and hung up. The hospital was only eight blocks away, but she never showed up. So there it was. Her unmistakable indifference brought me to being able to see myself and the whole history of my denial. The one thing I could never have understood was that she didn't care. But we cannot expect to understand others' motives. We would only be lucky to do so. I suddenly recognized that I didn't need to let her determine my actions, as I had. I had an unlimited right to make my own decision. That was to get out of the situation by divorcing her. The divorce gave me hell too, but it was a cleaner hell than what came before. Rage and fear and despair gradually left me because I had decided, finally, to follow my own star.

BEACH REFLECTION NO. 26

To sit by the sea did not protect the beachcomber from depression. The beauty and drama of the shore sometimes washed past, not into, him. Depression, he knew, often was only anger in disguise. An anger aimed at himself and his blunders or emotional blindnesses. As each roller washed onto the beach, it would reinforce how each error washed through his memory. Splash, the overweening anger when he threatened to chop off his wife's lover's head, for God's sake; splash, his wussy unwillingness to send his unfaithful wife packing; splash, his failure to leave behind two lovers who clearly did not want permanent relationships; splash, and on and on went his self-condemnations. They were many and crowded about his memory like a sea filled with parasites.

Then he saw a trio of brown pelicans dropping like fighter planes into the waves, to rise again, circle and dive, again, thrusting their necks deep into the surf. First, he smiled at the rhythm of it, then laughed at their singular unity of motion and purpose. They had much to do and were doing it. Not for them came worries of past and future. Just the active life of purpose, focus, and needs of the present.

Perhaps they had learned to fish from past mistakes. Perhaps, even now, not every plunge caught a perch, but for them, perhaps, a miss made the next strike more precise.

The beachcomber realized that the same was true for his own checkered life of errors. He had done as much as possible to correct them. At times he made attempts to make up for them; at other times he just left them behind and moved on. Other times he had to just let them lie, done and over.

As he watched the pelicans, he remembered the call from his daughter. She had been remembering too. For her, though, it was about all the ways he had shown her how to cope with her own physical crises. His example, she said, filled her with admiration for how he had worked through all the terrible times he had faced. She thanked him, now, in case she had not remembered to do that before.

With that thought, his heart came back into the present–the birds, the surf, the twinkling, spray-ridden air.

HAIKU NO. 27

On a broken branch
sits a tattered chickadee.
Only the wind sings.

CHAPTER 29

Three Principles of Living Relationships

I CAME AWAY FROM DIVORCE no. 1 with a few ideas that were new, at least to me:

1. It takes two hands to clap. Don't worry; I will explain.
2. I am not my partner's keeper. This one may be more obvious.
3. Both partners are free to choose how they will live. This was the hardest one to learn.

Anyone who believes and lives by these principles of marriage could be described as an existentialist. To be an existentialist is to have a clear path for decision making. That is good, because anyone involved in a troubled marriage is going to have a lot of decisions to make. Few situations cloud the mind so completely. That's when experience-based principles can be of most help.

1. ONE HAND CAN'T CLAP.

No matter what I tried, I could not keep my marriage. The recognition hit me that two people cannot keep a relationship unless they both choose to do so. To make it simple for myself, I made up a metaphor based on my theater experiences: "One hand can't clap; it takes two hands." Just try to clap with one hand. A little air may move, but nothing more. It's the same for a couple: one person leans in with love, and the other walks away. No argument, no persuasion, and indeed no force can make the other person stay with you if they don't choose to. I tried every method of keeping my marriage that was suggested in the book I consulted on the subject. My actions and words moved some air around but never reached her ears. She never explained how she came to be indifferent to me. Whatever it was, I may have moved some air with my speeches or gestures, but I never moved her. Despite my three-year struggle to keep my marriage, what I really needed to learn from her was this: "Do you want to keep our marriage?" Even more importantly, I needed to ask myself that question. Had I focused on that, the time I spent pleading, crying, confronting, and rationalizing could have been cut down enormously. It seems odd to me, now, that I never thought of it. I would say to myself, "Why is she doing this to me?" Well, she wasn't doing it to me; she was doing it for her own reasons. A question more to the point would be, "In the face of her behavior, what do I want for myself?" That question would have dispelled all my confusion. Instead, I kept wondering why she was sticking with her affair. These many years later I still don't know why she began and continued her affair right into marrying the guy. What I concluded was that I couldn't bear the punishment my children and I were enduring, so I pushed for a divorce. Marriage vows hold a beautiful promise, but we never promised to be unhappy or even desperate in that marriage. That makes it all the more important for a spouse to participate at least enough to let you know how she is feeling about your marriage. If she is not present with you, your attempt to touch hands comes to nothing. Now it helps me to remember that one hand can't clap. That is the first great existential conclusion

I drew from my first divorce. It has given me an essential clarity about relationships ever since. I have learned to remember that I may control my own hand but not the other person's hand. Therefore, I must pay attention to my own hand and what choices it has for where to clap. In other words, let yourself "communicate with the other person, but continually consult your own needs."

2. I AM NOT MY PARTNER'S KEEPER.

Now I will begin to describe the second conclusion I drew. Mysterious little myths threaded throughout our culture open weak areas in our hearts, sometimes. For men, one of these myths is that someday we will run into the gorgeous woman who will spontaneously leap to give us the most incredible sex possible. For such a gift, we will incur no obligation. For women, it is that someday they might just meet the ideal man, the prince who will completely understand and adore them. Only then will they stop keeping their options open in relationships with men. Such myths tend to encourage us to keep our relationships tentative. Once I discovered that a dear male friend of mine was having an affair. When I asked him if he loved her, he said, "Larry, you always fall in love." I think he lived the male myth.

3. SO HERE IS MY THIRD REALIZATION:

"Both partners are free to choose how they will live."

I cannot repeat this too often: I have to grant my partner equal freedom to stay or go as she likes. I ask only that she keeps me informed as to how our marriage is going for her. Another of my favorite sayings is, "I have enough trouble managing my own life, much less trying to manage someone else's life." Oh, I'm as willing as anyone to offer advice. But I've never been able to lie to myself well enough to pass over my own serious errors of judgment. If I tried to guide others I would then become responsible for their mistakes as well as my own. I don't want the responsibility. Even further, my own life has convinced me utterly that my world is different from everyone else's world. Every time I learned that my wife was with her lover, I would pace up and down and say loudly to myself, "Why is she doing this to me?" I can't account for why it was so hard for me to switch from thinking she was doing it to me to realizing she wasn't doing it to me at all. In fact, she was doing it with him. She had made her own choice, and now it was time for me to make mine. Therefore, I have learned to be a partner, not a keeper. Each spouse bears the total freedom to choose life, and we stay together voluntarily or not at all.

BEACH REFLECTION NO. 27

The best time to sit by the sea was during the long drawing out of the tide. The ebb left more and more of the shore exposed. Little gullies appeared to drain backwaters. Small hillocks between rivulets lay like wrinkles on an old face.

He contemplated them as with everything else, past and present. One thing he knew: you never stopped wondering why you had made the mistakes you did.

Why did he wait to get old to know that we are not only free to choose our own lives, values, and beliefs, but we become most effective and most mature when we do so?

His divorces had hurt, but what a relief it had been to be free of the need to condemn and blame his former wives. How could he blame them for choosing to live some other way? Would he be happier now with a woman who didn't really give a hoot about him and maybe even never had? Women have complete freedom to have their lives the way they need to be. So did he. He had learned to accept that principle completely.

Life came at you like endless rollers, some larger, some smaller. All hit the beach, lifted the sand, swirled, and sank back in regression. While it soothed, sometimes he had to get up and scramble away or be drenched. Sometimes he got drenched, anyway. That was life.

HAIKU NO. 28

Lovers seek for dunes
to embrace in their rolled depths.
Sand holds no secrets.

CHAPTER 30

Divorce No. 2: New Marriage, New Mistakes

ONE TRIES NOT TO MAKE the same mistakes in a second marriage as in the first. Too bad that intention does not guarantee against a whole new set of mistakes.

For example, my first marriage contained little sexual pleasure. A key event in that effect came during the first year of that marriage. One morning, my wife broke out in tears. When I asked her what was wrong, she said, "I'm either in the bedroom or the kitchen." I took her to mean that I was overly demanding in the bedroom, as a newlywed might expect to be. Without a further discussion that someone less inclined to take blame on himself might have, I backed off my activity. From then on, Kinsey would have placed our sexual activity in the lower third of his survey.

By the time we divorced, twenty years later, I had found little relief from my needs in a few acts of embarrassing sexual harassment and one extramarital affair. My wife never knew of that affair when it occurred, largely, I suppose, because she had little need for such intimacy. By the time we got a divorce, I spilled over with sexual energy, or I never would have entered into my next relationship and marriage so energetically.

Though she was intellectually and artistically gifted, her background could not have been more different than mine. To simplify, my father was an educator; hers was a farmer who became wealthy. I had become a college teacher; for many years she described herself as a "dirt hippie."

Despite my sense of our differences, my urges drove me to the point where I ignored any glaring warnings. I lived rather neatly; her house was a mess. My children were middle class; her child, to be honest and far too late for honesty, struck me immediately as trouble. I felt an instant sense of repulsion. My first and biggest error was in not immediately breaking off our relationship. I have no excuse or any reasonable way to explain how or why my reaction to the boy was so intense. No matter. There was no way for me to be fair to him or his mother because I just instinctively felt that way. Worse yet, I never told her. Like other fools in lust, I passed over the truth. It seems to me now to be a weak defense of myself that during the next eight years I parented him to the best of my ability.

Naturally, the boy himself did not constitute the whole challenge. Unlike me, his mother was a permissive parent who rarely exerted herself to give guidance to her son. Her permissiveness counteracted my own attempt to take authoritative charge when necessary. For example, when we were called down to deal with his arrest by police, she at first refused to go. "I just can't," she cried. "I can't face it." I made her go. No other approach would be responsible. We often came down on different sides in parenting issues. Rule No. 1: don't marry someone whose parenting style conflicts with yours. You will only cancel each other out, and the child loses.

Perhaps the timing of our relationship also worked against us. In the background of our new relationship, my vision loss accelerated so that I was making a career change, learning to use a white cane and letting go of driving my car. Years later she wrote that she regretted not being more understanding while all that happened. The trouble with regrets is that by their very nature, they come too late.

Our first few years bubbled with joy like a freshly poured glass of champagne. Still, I was looking for stability of mood in daily life, and she ran an emotional gambit rather constantly. My greater vulnerability gradually led me to become somewhat defensive about sex, travel, and even mealtimes. Often, I felt attacked, as when she told me how irritating it was that I bought a horse and horned in on what had been her activity; that is, horseback riding.

Earlier, when I pointed out that one of my needs was affection, I could have understood better what was missing in our relationship on such occasions as this: I would meet her when she came home from work. I would get up, reach for a hug, and have her push me away. "Don't be so gooey," she would say. By the end of our eight years we had gotten into the habit of making constant sarcastic rejoinders at each other. Once, her sister told us that made her uncomfortable. A couple of nights she came home late from hanging around in a bar. Once she had to push free of an importunate man on her way home. Clearly, our tie was weakening. She has pointed out that a major reason was that we had little or no sex for the final six months before we both began extramarital affairs.

My view of my second marriage probably bears no relationship to my second wife's understanding. How could it turn out any other way given our differences in family background, style of past life, and parenting conflicts? My experience was that she was too hard on me. At the end I told her that she had been "too much, too often, and for too long." Perhaps what she needed was a man with a stronger character than mine. I would like to have remained married. Each divorce constitutes a sense of failure, a loss of self-confidence in one's ability to cope, and a drop into depression.

Did our extramarital affairs end our marriage? Only as the visible manifestation of our emotional separation. Our togetherness had been eroding for months. Deep down, I believe we both were looking for a way out. I think, now, that we both recognized insoluble differences. Neither of us retained the energy to discuss or negotiate those differences. And perhaps they had been too extreme from the beginning to bridge our cultural and emotional gaps. No doubt many spouses use affairs to escape an unsatisfactory marriage. Still, that habit demonstrates my thesis that if we understood ourselves properly, we could pull up our socks and say directly to our partners, "Sorry, honey, but I don't want this marriage anymore." Then we would save our useless sexual misadventure for when we became single again. That would be cleaner and more mature, more what we should live up to.

BEACH REFLECTION NO. 28

The shore lay still and hot, a rare experience on Washington beaches. The beachcomber slipped off his usual jacket and rolled up his sleeves. Small wavelets barely disturbed the sands when they washed up onto the sand so lazily. What he especially began to notice was the wild flickering of sunlight off ripples, like silver lures following trolling boats. A swath of flashing lay down between him and the sun. He fell into a mesmerized state, falling further and further away into his past until he contacted his original epiphany of light with the consultant Len Clark.

The light of the past and present filled him, held him in a richly joyous suspension. Is this how champagne feels when freshly poured, how the first cool breeze feels at the end of a hot day, or what the first kiss of love does to you?

He could only hope that this was the light that waited for him after he died.

HAIKU NO. 29

Only a black bear
no larger than a small man
shot by a small man.

CHAPTER 31

Marriage No. 3: One Way to Find a Permanent Relationship

IT IS A FUNNY THING that we humans can go through childhood, adulthood, and parenting without becoming mature. Oh, I have met a few youngsters who started life as mature beings. They are rare. Many wives I know feel they are raising three children, and one of them is their husband. These influences have led me to believe that maturity relates to the acceptance of responsibility for doing what is necessary before following any recreational impulses.

In terms specifically of relationships, maturity lies in living by my three principles: it takes two hands to clap, I am not my partner's keeper, and every individual is free to choose his or her own life's path. I don't think I had fully internalized those principles until I had reached my late fifties. I wrote this book to encourage people to reach maturity as I describe it much earlier than I did. In that late period I dated a woman who eventually convinced me she could not be one of the hands that would clap, and that she could not merge the needs of her life with mine. Despite the effort I had put into that relationship, it came easily to me to let it go. In the past I had tried to force relationships to merge; now I knew better. The end came comfortably this time.

That set the stage for my daughter's intervention in my life. She bought me a gift membership in eHarmony, a web-based service whose purpose is to match couples into long-term relationships. The site opened with an important question and followed with a two-hour examination of the member's needs, interests, and values. For the first time in my life I was asked what three things I needed most in a partner. Why had I never done that before I even began looking for partners? It suddenly seemed like the obvious thing to do.

After much thought, I wrote that I needed someone who was capable of forming long-term attachments, a good conversationalist, and an affectionate nature. Neither of my two spouses or three lovers possessed all three of those qualities. The front-end test of eHarmony really woke me up to my own needs.

In the course of examining the candidates listed by the service, I finally ran into my third wife, JoAnne. Not only did she possess all three qualities, but we meshed in many ways: social background, love of reading, commitment to finding the right person and not going through another failed marriage, and so forth. We held many three-hour phone conversations before we ever met. To be blunt, when we met, we already knew a great deal about each other.

Think of the contrast between that and how relationships usually occur. You meet someone. You like them for their looks or for their manner and expressions, or for some perceived connection such as type of work. You have coffee. You think things go well, so you arrange a date. This process continues until you might even become intimate, but it could be a year or even longer before you discover something about the person you just can't stand. You break up or divorce and feel angry or disappointed. Why did all this happen, perhaps over and over again? That is all you can expect when you begin in ignorance and meet only in ideal and well-prepared-for situations. You focus on the good experiences and gloss over disturbing indications. After all, many a likeable person doesn't wish for permanence; many a person has the social skills to be engaging during a date or fun activity. What we need is to have an argument of some kind. That's when you really see more deeply into a person. The real question underneath all long-term relationships is can you both work through difficulties to an accommodation. That is what we need to know, and what is so hard to find out.

So here I am, finally, in a marriage with a woman who has all the qualities I have needed all my life. We even read occasional books together so we can discuss them. We talk so deeply as we drive that we arrive at our destinations long before we expect to. She accepts my health crises because we have so much that is good, together. I accept her occasional frustration or anger outbursts because of her deeply honest and direct character. There is no game-playing between us. I admire her skill and dedication to counted cross-stitch; she likes my writing. Best of all, she laughs at my jokes.

When you approach it maturely, love can indeed be a many-splendored thing.

POEM NO. 2: MY PROPOSAL TO JOANNE

SPINDRIFT

Caught in a spindrift of love,
I wink at the clamor of waves
and smile as pelicans dive.

I love you like the weave and weft of clouds,
the way sun dazzle lights the waves,
or how beach birds dance in spreading tide.

I love you to every horizon
with all its soaring gulls,
loafing sea lions, fishing boats,
and all the odors of salt and life.

Take this ring with my pledge
to love you this way as long as sun,
sand, surf, and beach abide.

PART 6

Experience Is a Hard School

BEACH REFLECTION NO. 29

Not all lies still on the beach. Not the quietude of the ebb tide, or even the rare windless morning. Not the beauty of the shore drew him outward from his dark thoughts on this day, and, he remembered, on other days as well. Too many bad events conspired to sabotage any present satisfaction.

The beachcomber could recount every terrible and terrifying event of his life. A bad memory would hit and make him grunt in dismay. He couldn't justify himself at any point, much less drag his memory away. Each dark experience appeared like a hand plunged through the surface of the sea into his illusory underwater serenity. Out of nowhere what some people called "reality" would slam his heart and life until he almost blanked out with despair. He didn't like to think of only terrible events as reality. He wanted to think of good times as reality too, but the pain, the impact of each crisis, did seem to power his reactions more than good times.

He could list them, from his high school girlfriend making out with another guy, to losing two jobs and being sent on active duty as out of nowhere, to being caught making a fake ID for a shipmate. All that happened before he was twenty-two. God. How those events had hurt. Yet now he knew they were nothing to what was coming.

The difference between them and his later life was that later crises kept on revealing consequences long after the immediate crisis. He had ignored all warnings that his first job was in jeopardy, that he had married a woman who never loved him, or that his health was neither stable nor focused on a single disease. His lack of awareness of impending trouble made the loss of his first job a terrible shock. For a time he lay stunned in emotional immobility. His wife said he had not smiled for months. Even worse, he struggled with the consequences for three years afterward as he finally forced himself to write and finish his doctoral dissertation and relearned college teaching methods. He had been lazy before losing his job, he acknowledged. Perhaps he could gather some pride by how thoroughly he had addressed his weaknesses after losing his job. There was a modicum of success in that, after all, and in time life got better.

That was at least true until the next manure storm swept through. After being a part-time teacher for three years, he got a good job in an interesting community. Still, he admitted to himself that he arrived at his new job regretting having left behind a love affair. He knew it had been the best thing to do, but a sadness often drew him to a scenic overlook for sorrowful reflections. That feeling passed.

Even with a good job, life gave nothing but a punctuated equilibrium. In a few years Crohn's disease put him in the hospital. A few years later came his first divorce. He got past the illness, but the divorce didn't go away because it separated him from his children. How could any man be happy to be with his children only two weekends a month? Now those are endless consequences of the sort called "reality," as in the saying, "Reality bites."

Like a new job, his new relationship promised a return to happiness and comfort. Even now he had not become acclimated to the certainty of the next crisis. Through blindness and accompanying discrimination, he changed his career from college teaching to management of disability services. In a few more years his marriage declined into divorce, and he left his management job for parts unknown.

Of course, there were healthy aspects to making a complete break with his past, but he was unemployed for two years. The crisis that arrived then was not his own but serious enough. His brother's girlfriend committed suicide. He was not surprised at the terrible consequences her act had on his brother. He, himself, had years ago rejected suicide as an alternative due to its dire impact on everybody else. Not only that, he knew it as a permanent solution to a temporary problem. Once his brother was through the worst of the crisis, the beachcomber finally found a new job in management and renewed his hope for the future.

He guessed later that he had never fit in with the self-serving culture of the management, so in a few years they let him go. In a mixture of anger and relief he took another job for six months. Not only did he not care for the people or the work, he contracted drug-induced lupus. Finally, he gave up work and retired. It took time for him to admit that he no longer was healthy enough to perform an eight-hour workday.

God, such memories brought enough pain for one day. He shook his head. He took some deep breaths. Just in time, he saw his guide dog sit up and then lunge off toward a man with a dog approaching from the north. He just had time to renew his grip on the flexi-lead and lock it. Commodore's lunge nearly yanked the lead from his hand, but at least he had kept his dog from coming at the other beachcomber like an attack dog. Commodore was harmless, only enthusiastic, but how would a stranger know?

He smiled and waved at the man and his dog. No one could imagine that anyone could be on a crisp, rock-strewn beach and think the thoughts he had been thinking. He decided to stop thinking them. He had to face it: experience was a hard school, but he had learned in it. It had made him who he was.

HAIKU NO. 30

The rasp of a crow
echoes through groves of beach pines,
cries louder than surf.

CHAPTER 32

To Learn from Experience

BENJAMIN FRANKLIN WROTE, "EXPERIENCE IS a hard school, but a fool will learn in no other." I must disagree with the famous man: It is the fool who does not learn even from experience. A fool will ignore the way a specific experience contradicts his beliefs. The rest of us can learn lessons from experience. Even if we do learn from others, as Franklin suggests, we still must test what we know through our personal experiences.

You hear people swear they will never get over such and such a calamity. To hear them talk, you would think that learning from experience was the standard by which we live. The reality is that too many people live by fixed beliefs and attitudes that a train couldn't push aside.

What lies outside our consciousness comes to us via the narrow pipelines of vision, odor, taste, sensation, and hearing. We find it easy enough to set aside what our external awareness shows us to listen to that beloved inner voice. We humans have an immense capacity to believe. It is, after all, our inner voice that strikes us as our true comforter in all our most lonely, desolate moments. We humans have even shown that we can commit suicide in the belief that suicide is the path to the Hale-Bopp Comet or to heaven or paradise, if we just do it right. Suicide bombers, whatever their immediate motivations, clearly are driven by an expectation of a reward in the afterlife. Perhaps they prove only that it is easier to die for their beliefs than to live for them. I remember General Patton's famous speech to his troops that he didn't want them to die for their country; he wanted the other son of a bitch to die for his. I believe deeply that, tempted though we are by attractive beliefs, the more attractive because they are more internalized, we should examine what we believe as an ongoing process. In fact, I argue for a systematic way of thinking that cycles between what we experience and learn from things outside us and what we accept as beliefs inside us. A constant cycling between the outer and inner tends to be self-correcting. Not only do people have to let themselves see the implications of their experiences, they actually have to have a wide range of experiences upon which to judge. You can't be like my old landlord in Utah who told me African Americans were less intelligent than white Americans. I offered him some famous names. His response was that such examples of African Americans with significant accomplishments was that they had "white brains." There's a reason for the sardonic phrase, "Don't confuse me with facts; my mind's made up."

Some of us don't recognize or embrace our fundamental freedom to choose what we feel. We may not accept our right to revise our understanding in the light of new experiences or new sources of information. As Jack McDevitt wrote in his novel *Omega,*

> Somewhere we taught ourselves that our opinions are more significant than the facts. And somehow we get our egos and our opinions and Truth all mixed up in a single package, so that when something does challenge one

of the notions to which we subscribe,
we react as if it challenges us. (Cryptic
Inc., 2003, page 357)

I doubt anyone would paint themselves purple and then commit suicide had they allowed knowledge of the spatial mechanics of cometary motion to penetrate their minds. They actually committed their very existence to a phantom of faith, one that few people could even imagine believing. As Mr. Spock was fond of saying in *Star Trek*, "Nothing unreal exists."

A way to deal with our beliefs is to let our range of life experiences come to mind.

Being present in the moment, smelling the roses, tasting the wine, and acknowledging the gift of affection from loved ones and friend keeps us prepared to evaluate the truths by which we live. The first trick is to see. The second is to accept. Our sense of wonder, can we sustain it throughout life, keeps us seeing. The second part is to work at understanding what we see. Basic to all this is to allow ourselves to think for ourselves rather than adhere to any of the many dogmas our social environment seems to try to force on us. We must try to cling to self-determination and an ongoing process of checking our perceptions.

For example, Even though the destruction of the Twin Towers fits the description of a catastrophe, such attacks will never be commonplace enough to directly threaten all those who remain terrified by the event. We are much more likely to die in a car accident than by a terrorist act. I remember how few Americans I ran into in my 1987 visit to England. In one shop, a British man asked me, "Where are all the Americans?" I told him I guessed many stayed home because they expected there would be terrorist reprisals because we launched our attack on Libya from Britain. In fact, one of my college colleagues had canceled his family's trip to England for that reason. The man said, rather indignantly, "We don't have that sort of thing here." Whether that was true or not, the man had a good point. I had a very uncrowded and peaceful visit to England that year. The Libyans did not attack England then or ever.

I witnessed the IRA attack on the London Postal Tower in 1971. I watched from the Academy Hotel as pieces fell from the tower. I was there, yet, London is a vast city, and few people who lived or visited London at the time recognized any danger to themselves. Any fear we may feel about the risks of terrorist attacks may focus on the danger to our countrymen and even to our economy, but our personal danger from such events is completely random. We can adjust our sense of endangerment accordingly, but only if we let our minds accept the possibility that we are free to check our reaction against the reality around us. Please understand that I do not dismiss serious emotional reactions to 9/11. My own son left the second tower before it was hit, and he had to run many blocks through the explosion of a cloud of dust and debris from the collapsing building. During the following months, he gave interviews on national television to tell how he had seen several people jump from the towers. He remembered every article of clothing they wore. He saw one of the security guards who guided people from the building later carried out on a stretcher. He experienced what happened at the Twin Towers as a war zone, and he will never forget the images burned on his soul. He has every right to live in fear of further terrorism, but he faces more immediate challenges.

If we are able to remember the previous attempt to destroy the towers in 1991, we could understand the disaster at the World Trade Center within a larger context.

Some of us who are old enough remember the rash of bank bombings in the 1960s. We may remember the raid on the bomb-making facilities of the Weathermen. Add in the bombing of the federal building in Oklahoma City, and we will see that terrorism in America is by no means either unique or limited to Islamic terrorists. In other words, terrorist attacks have a history in the United States. Bombings exist far more frequently in other countries, perhaps. We live in a world where these things happen, but remembering that can help reduce our fear to a level equivalent to our fear of automobile accidents. That is, we can adjust our fear of terrorist activities to a background buzz rather than something that allows us to go along with an unprovoked attack on a country that never had attacked us or even sponsored any kind of terrorism directed at us. A sense of unreasonable fear disturbs our ability to make sensible decisions either for ourselves or for our nation.

One event doesn't necessarily create a life lived in fear. For example, once, as a child, I was caught in an elevator above the finished floors of a high-rise. I jumped up and down in rage until the elevator slipped free and went back down. My biggest fear was being caught for playing in the elevator. Many years later, on another elevator, a woman said to a friend that her son still fears elevators since the day he was stuck in one as a child. I wanted to tell her that I had been so stuck and wasn't afraid. Maybe there was some other reason for her son's formless fear of elevators. New rides in elevators should have long ago cured her son of any further fear of being stuck in an elevator. The best way to deal with traumas is to overlay them with new experiences. However, that only works if we learn from experience.

Perhaps another explanation of why some people hold on to self-defeating beliefs is simply out of habit. Once I asked a dear friend why she was about to marry another alcoholic, her third. She said, "Larry, it's what I'm familiar with. I speak alcoholism." I conclude from her words that people are more fearful of unfamiliar risks than familiar ones. To some, distant danger ranks higher than something more immediate, such as known risks of car accidents within ten miles of our own homes. Take up self-knowledge from childhood and even young adult experiences, mix it with feedback from others, and you get a chance to guide your life more advantageously. Try to sideslip both inner and outer knowledge, and become a complete fool. To be a fool is a choice we don't really want to make, for foolish acts have consequences that don't disappear overnight.

Let me adapt another common saying: "Opinions are like, um, noses; everyone has one." The trouble is that not all opinions are equal. Some opinions have consideration of evidence backing them, while others offer only assertions without reference to proof. These latter believe something "just because." You can't gather three people in one room and have them completely agree on any single viewpoint. The joke goes that when two Jews come together you have three opinions. The rest of us want to know why Joe believes as he does.

Our opinions need to reflect who we are and how we behave. To do otherwise is to practice hypocrisy. We all know congressmen whose voting record differs from the content of their speeches; ministers whose sexual misbehavior escapes to the tabloids, actors proclaiming a product they don't use, or people who attack books they haven't read. Such people seem to consider opinions as lying outside the reality in which they actually live.

Many of us pretend to beliefs that allow us to slide by any rough spots showing what our real opinions may cause. That is fine, really, because it is much worse to delude ourselves than to delude others. However, to delude others often brings us into an uncomfortable conflict. Sometime along the way we will be pressed to act on what we didn't really believe, and that hurts.

We humans can wear many faces, live comfortably

in many houses. As Red Buttons said, "A house divided is a condominium." One reason no one can be labeled by their race or ethnicity is because we are all a kind of condominium of attitudes, experiences, and beliefs.

Not only do we wear many faces, we also go through passages of life when our opinions shift because the ground we stand on shifts. For example, Larry may have allegiances to many unities at the same time, and so can Jo Anne. He may be loyal to the Elks, his country, his country club, his children, and his profession; Jo Anne may have allegiance to her family, her thread shop, the company she works for, and a defined sense of right and wrong. No one could be surprised at what multiple beings we are, showing different personal styles to boys, bankers, bosses, and brothers. To keep a humorous slant on human varieties, a laconic Monty Python situation showed a gorilla applying for a job at a library. The librarian expressed regret that the gorilla didn't get the job because they needed someone with more teeth. The gorilla exclaims in frustration, "If I'd just known that, I would have applied as myself." Then the gorilla pulled off his gorilla head and showed that he was, in fact, a wolf.

Tell the truth, now: how many of us apply for jobs

as ourselves? How many of us date as ourselves? How many of us talk to our ministers, rabbis, or priests as ourselves? Point made. A dear friend of mine quietly told me one day during a break in play rehearsals that he had eight children, all of whom were very worried about the state of his soul. He said they viewed him as a Mormon patriarch, but that he had passed through so many types of faith in his life that he no longer cared to hide his current view of religion. I asked him what that was. He said, "It sure upset them when I told them not to come to my funeral because I won't be there."

My conclusion is that not only do we contain varieties of allegiances, but they change throughout our lives. To ignore that is to be inhuman.

BEACH REFLECTION NO. 30

No ocean beach is quiet. Steady breezes, shifting sand, bird cries, and the rhythmic pounding of heavy surf make it nearly impossible to speak with anyone not very near. And yet it is that seashore itself that speaks. Its array of voices often wipe away all human sounds, those human sounds that so confuse and mystify the beachcomber.

Yet interruptions walked down off the dune onto the sand and confronted the beachcomber. This particular man, dressed in street clothes and with wind whipping his dark hair, asked how much of the dune had been washed away by rough tides this winter.

"Do you think the water will reach my house and wash it away?"

It is hard to be honest when faced with a question like that. In the first place, the beachcomber hoped the house, built rashly on the top of the dune, actually would wash away. He felt angry that his community and people possessing more money than they could use wisely built homes along the dune. Not only were the homes not safe, they intruded on the beneficial isolation and serenity of the meeting place of sand, sea, and sky.

But the beachcomber held to the courtesies with which he had lived, so assured the man that he doubted the tide would wash away all the dune, even though it had probably already pulled twenty feet of it away.

The man nodded and struggled back up the steep dune to his house. The incident left the beachcomber to wonder what the real nature of truth was.

HAIKU NO. 31

His dog tried to roll
in the stink of a dead fish.
Here, life and death meet.

CHAPTER 33

The Pitfalls of Language

With words we sugarcoat our nastiest motives
and our worst behavior, but with words we also
formulate our highest ideals and aspirations.
—S. I. Hayakawa, *Language in
Thought and Action*, preface

A FISH MAY BE AS unaware of its watery environment
as we are of the sea of words that drench us all
day and every day. Words pour from every stereo,
television, radio, diners at our own or the next table,
newspapers or magazines on the waiting room's table,
our ministers, coaches, teachers, parents, and even
informational messages on our phones while we are
on hold. All these are messages to get us to buy, to

adopt, to reject, or to act in ways preferred by the originators of the endless messages.

Do all these messages change our behavior? You bet they do. Candidates for office who spend the most money on advertising most often get the office. Advertisers wouldn't invest millions in Super Bowl television ads unless they brought in sales to compensate them for the expenditure. Did news that salmonella infected broccoli reduce the broccoli market? You bet it did. Did some people believe the current Health Reform Bill contained "death panels?" For sure they did, despite that the idea was a complete fabrication. There are even people who believe there was no Holocaust just because some source said so.

Mind you, a lot of useful information also comes along with the rushing tide of words that engulf us. The difficulty is to know which words are truer than others, which are more false than true, and which are outright lies. Who has time for all that?

There is an answer to that question, and it lies in ourselves.

One thing we can do is live by the familiar phrase, "Consider the source." If the speaker or writer is a person, we want to know the person possesses legitimate expertise; if a news source, we want to see specific names of sources of information; if a movie or radio program, we need to determine whether we are seeing entertainment or specific facts. If we read or hear something that does not at times violate our own view of things, we are probably not ranging far enough afield from our own comfort zone.

For example, conservatives seem to believe that public radio is too liberal, while liberals feel it is too conservative. I take those contradictory reactions as a sign that public radio is a reliable source of information. On the other hand, everyone knows that Fox News is expressly a right-wing conservative network, sometimes on the extreme right.

As each of us passes through our lives, we learn that some sources do badly by us and others give us more dependable views. A degree of skepticism makes us prepared to question the validity of the speech that comes at us from all sides. "Don't believe everything you hear" is a good way to begin. Balancing a number of different sources is an even better idea.

The best thing to do is to decide whether we will come to conclusions on a rational or an irrational basis. Jonathan Swift had it right when he observed that man is not a rational being, but a rationalizing being. He meant that we humans are more likely to use our minds to make things fit our expectations than to entertain contrary information. We base most of our conclusions on emotional reactions, not on a consideration of evidence. Let us call emotional reactions "confirmation bias." This means that we tend to recognize and agree only with information supporting what we already believe. That, of course, is how we win arguments. That is, if your purpose is to win an argument.

What if we wish to learn instead of win? How do we shift from confirming our biases to opening our minds to perspectives other than our own?

As an example, once I began an argument with an Orthodox Jew. I told her I couldn't understand how anyone could be orthodox. I believed that orthodoxy indicated a conformity to established beliefs. To me, at that time, conformity meant that such a person had not examined her beliefs. The woman did not take my attack personally. She spoke seriously: "You can't have reforming or alternate viewpoints if you don't have an orthodoxy to react to. There's no reason to think that a thoughtful person could not choose to be orthodox." We must have discussed the subject for half an hour, and the result was I changed my mind. I came to understand how someone could be orthodox without being brain-dead.

I believe that to function well in life we have to

be able to see and understand opposing viewpoints. How else can we deal with them?

During the heated political climate we now call Watergate, my college wanted to set up a public panel discussion of that issue and the Nixon administration specifically. No faculty member volunteered to represent the Nixon administration. Without that, no debate could occur. Finally they asked me to do it. Now, I am proud to be a liberal. Look up the word in any dictionary, and you will see what being liberal means to me. In order to let the panel go ahead, I agreed to act as the defender of the Nixon administration. After a slow start, proceedings were interrupted by two people pouring vilification on my head. After the initial shock, all I could say to them was that I preferred not to have either of them to be the leaders of our nation. They made me afraid for my physical safety. Even Nixon was more level-headed than were they.

What I learned was how dangerous immoderate opposition blocks understanding. Nothing good can come out of hate.

When Dr. Benjamin Spock wrote about child development, he spoke as an authority in his field. When he spoke against the Vietnam War, his was just another citizen's opinion. I do not believe a speaker or writer is an authority just because I agree with him. Nor do I accept his viewpoint because he is famous.

In another example, I could more readily begin to worry about a movement called a one world order if I could identify anyone, anywhere, who either had the power or the desire to bring us all together in a one world order. I do my best to stay informed from various sources, and what I see worldwide are tribes, ethnicities, and other kinds of groups trying to separate from their larger countries. Southern Sudan seeks independence from northern Sudan. Basques struggle to break away from Spain. Kurds fight to form their own state.

There must be writers who work to convince people that such a drive toward a one world order exists, but where do they get the idea? And who are those who believe their words? I can only call such a phenomenon the fascination of the snake. What happens is someone makes claims so scary, so bizarre, and so threatening that we can't take our eyes off it. That is the way many of us look at a snake we've suddenly discovered by our feet. However, with our eyes fixated on the bizarre claims, we tend not to look aside at other viewpoints, ones with more actual authority in the field of world affairs.

Then, there is name-calling. To call anyone a

name is to simplify who they are to an impossible, and usually incorrect, degree. Some call a political opponent a "socialist." If it were true, that person would be trying to get the government to take control of the means of production or capital of the country. This happened in Venezuela and Russia in terms of their oil production but has not happened in the United States, nor will it. We are not talking here about emergency measures a country might take to prevent economic collapse. That is not socialism, but an attempt to prevent the collapse of a capitalistic economy. Many men call someone a bastard whose parent were quite legitimately married. Once, while I was in the navy, I jokingly called a man a son of a bitch. He got angry and aggressive. He said, "Don't you talk about my mother like that." To him, the name was not a joke, and the truth is that name-calling is never a joke. It is a kind of lie.

Once, as I walked across a footbridge, a young man rode by on a bicycle and called me a "fag." I can only think he thought I was weird for guiding myself with a white cane. Name-calling is about hurting someone's feelings, not about accuracy. So it is with the word "fag." He didn't mean, I suppose, that I was gay, only weird. Yet why call anyone a fag? What if they are, in fact, gay? They may yet be parents, voters, chairmen of boards, line workers for the electric company, and good friends to many people. Every one of us is many things, not just one thing.

But, of course, name-calling is about hurting, or negatively labeling someone to put them down. Truth is not at issue. We should not give credence to any writer or speaker who calls other people names, or if the purpose is just to slant our opinions without offering any dependable viewpoint. As Martin Luther King said, the important thing is the content of a person's character.

To be a rational, rather than rationalizing, being, it's best to test our beliefs against actual evidence. Evidence lies not with emotion or opinion, but in facts that can be verified by the simple act of checking the sources.

As an example, take the belief of some that the Holocaust never happened. Any check of archives reveals the usual German thoroughness of record-keeping. Medical experimentation, for one activity in prison camps, lays open names and dates and experiments attempted and their results. There can be no doubt these experiments actually took place. They are extensively documented.

We also need to consider the plausibility of charges made or unusual claims made. Is it plausible that General Patton was killed by Communists? Is it plausible to paint a Hitler moustache on a portrait of President Obama? Think of how many people would have to be involved to hide an alien flying machine in Area 51 or any other location. It's hard for two people to keep a secret, much less dozens of people. Many claims we read or hear simply do not meet the plausibility test.

Finally, we need to learn how to recognize and discount emotional appeals.

When we use emotionally loaded words, the emotion we are trying to arouse is obvious. Yet many people do not recognize that what they are reading or hearing is emotion, not truth. What emotion tells us is how the speaker or writer feels about a subject; the emotion provides no other information.

What we look for is actual, qualified authorities for believable information and trust relatively emotion-free language for content worth considering.

We are least likely to think critically when we encounter statements we already believe. It's a way of keeping a closed mind to be sure to read only those sources that say what we already believe.

There are other cautions about the words that come at us. It's one thing to be stubborn and another to be firm; one thing to be an administrative assistant and another to be a secretary or clerk; one thing to be a Bible thumper and another to be an ordained minister. The words we use reflect our purposes but not necessarily the truth. You can always recognize an authentic authority. He or she will always identify sources on which an argument is based. Any reader could check the sources to establish the validity of the author's viewpoint.

What I want for all of us is to become crap detectors. A whole lot of fecal matter flies out of the hot-air propellers that surround us. To ask ourselves, "How do they know?" is the most reasonable response to those who direct their opinions and judgments at us. Not only do we want some substantiation of a political argument, we want to hear the voice of someone who has carefully considered the subject at hand. It's easy to recognize heated emotional verbiage. We recognize it because it tends to make us emotional as well. I say, do not believe any speaker who resorts to name-calling, such as with hot-button words such as "socialism," "Hitlerism," "Jack-booted thugs," or "radical," "rag-head," or any other such term. Really, any person who attacks the individual instead of the issue at hand should be a red light to the crap detector. It's what people do or say that matters in any debate, not their selfhood.

It is also well to remember that those with jobs in radio or television are entertainers. Their income depends entirely on keeping their audience. If their ratings fall, they fall. That is the definition of an entertainer. We must not think of them as truth-givers, philosophers, or authorities on any subject. We must not believe what they say just because they say it. There simply is no doubt they speak as they do to hold up their popularity ratings. The other thing is that they find invective and slander to be very popular with elements of the public. A crowd will always gather to witness a fight, always slow up to see an accident, or spend hours watching the trial of a famous man accused of murdering his ex-wife. Conflict is food to those of us who are bored, or those of us who feel inferior and look for someone to blame for all that is wrong with our lives. We may be impressed by the speaker's ranting; he may make us afraid of the scenarios he presents, but if we sit back and ask, "How does he know?" or "What evidence does he offer," we will see the emptiness of the ranting. I say, enjoy the entertainment, but don't believe just because you enjoy it.

We all have opinions, but not all opinions are equal. We want those backed up with some expertise or use of evidence. In court, when there is a reasonable doubt of guilt, we find the accused innocent. Yet, in life, many of us will allow ourselves to believe things that in court we would doubt. Let us see the truth that some accusations are valid in the sense of a trial, and others are simply baloney.

If someone begins a sentence with the phrase, "The fact is," you can almost be sure they will complete the sentence with an opinion. Too many people confuse fact with opinion. A man says, "Doug cheated me." We know the man has expressed an opinion because the word, "cheater," is a judgment or emotional reaction. Did Doug get caught shuffling the cards to get a specific result during a card game? Did he sell the man a car that he said had no problems but in fact needed a valve job? Did Doug sell him a defective toy and refuse to take it back? What Doug did, when he did it, and how he did it will probably be facts. It is the nature of a fact that we can independently check it out.

I could tell you that the Grand Coulee Dam is the one most recently built in Washington State. If you checked it out, you would discover I was wrong. You get an e-mail message warning you that our Social Security funds are being used to pay the health care of our congressmen, but if you checked it out, you would also find out the statement was false. That is why we like to use facts in our speaking and writing: facts, first off, give the impression we are trying to tell the truth. Second of all, if we check out the facts given, we can actually find out for ourselves whether they are accurate.

When a speaker or writer offers a lot of facts, we have found a good way to know what we know. And what we don't know and can't know.

HAIKU NO. 32

After such pounding
nothing so old as a beach
alive with new birds.

HAIKU NO. 33

Where does a finch fly
when summer begins to wane?
leaves fly wild in wind

CHAPTER 34

Illustration of Fixed Beliefs

1. FAITH HEALING.

TAKE AN EXTREME EXAMPLE: SAY that you are a person of a certain kind of faith. You genuinely believe that given enough faith, God will heal your wounds and illnesses. Then one day, you break your leg. No one can foresee such an accident, yet suddenly you are completely immobilized. However, you decide the best approach is to pray. Then, to give prayer more power, you invite in those who share your faith to have a faith intervention. It is a lovely ceremony, and love and affection abound. There is a laying on of hands and anointing with holy oils. Yet time passes, and your leg continues not to work. Besides, it has become very painful. Now, of course, you know that God inflicted many trials on Job; you work to retain an optimistic outlook.

Here's the dilemma: what you believe isn't working. At least not in terms of fixing your leg. Others may praise you for your steadfastness, but they can walk. If you say to yourself, "Screw this, I'm going to get help from a doctor," your leg will get fixed, but what about your beliefs and those of your community of believers? So, to rid yourself of current pain and the possibility of never walking right again, you go to a doctor. Most likely, you get your leg set and cast. Perhaps you see an orthopedic surgeon. Time passes, and your leg actually heals, and you walk normally. You have taken an action that worked, but at the same time a splint has been driven into your belief system. The next time you are either sick or injured, it is easier to go to a doctor than before. That is because you succeeded with your first decision. One success leads to another. That is how we learn from experience. A fool, in contrast, clings to his faith healing belief. He does not get better. His faith is constant, and his friends praise him for it, but he cannot walk, or walks very poorly. Well, he can live with that. God will provide. Then another injury or dangerous illness shows up. He continues to cling to his beliefs as his body, and in a tracking pattern his way of life, continues into dysfunction. He may take himself all the way to death on that path. And that's how it is when a fool cannot learn from experience.

2. CREATIONISM.

It wasn't until 1656 that anyone arrived at the notion that God created the earth on the night before October 23, 4004 BCE. The idea appeared two thousand years after the compilation of the Old Testament. We can ask what Bishop James Ussher knew that no one before him knew. Bishop Ussher was a devoted Calvinist and primate of the Protestant Church of Ireland during the civil war that deposed Charles I of England. He also convened a group of churchmen, who published a diatribe against Catholicism, calling it "superstitious and idolatrous" and that to allow Catholics to "freely exercise their religion" would be a sin. It strains credulity that such a source could have initiated one of the most illogical and widespread controversies of the past two centuries. What greater evidence could we choose to illustrate how tenaciously people cling to completely arbitrary beliefs.

Some people find creationism comfortable because it makes we humans out to be special to God. Instead of checking our internally held belief with the outside world, we spurn all contradiction to hold on to our belief. If, in contrast, we let ourselves realize that more than half the world bases their ideas on other systems of belief, we may be able to accept some lesser urgency about our commitment to a literal interpretation of our Bible.

Some people go so far as to attack information that contradicts their own viewpoint. Some people believe that the bioscience theory of evolution poses an attack on creationism. I cannot understand why, because creationism lies in the subject area of theology, or perhaps folklore or myth, but evolution lies completely in the curriculum of science. Each subject area uses different methods of validating information. Therefore, to support our belief in creationism, we attack the theory of evolution. We say, "Look, the fossil record is incomplete." Of course it is. How could it not be when all fossils deteriorate in the earth? Archaeology is lucky to find what we do.

I say with complete confidence that no replicated scientific studies give evidential support to creationism. And why should it? The Christian Bible does not tell us how to breed sheep. Breeding sheep is a scientific study based in agricultural science. Similarly, the theory of evolution arises from generations of those who carefully observed nature.

Let me point out the obvious truth that we cannot prove the validity of creationism by disproving evolutionary theory. That approach is as ludicrous as arguing we could teach a horse to talk just because the Bible said we could. Creationism must be proven via its own supporting evidence, if it is to be proved at all. Debates over the validity of the theory of evolution are a completely different subject than creationism. Therefore, arguing for creationism, or intelligent design, by finding fault with evolution is not a valid argument. It may help to reverse the argument and attempt to prove the theory of evolution by the use of biblical authorities. Why would we bother?

A person can obviously choose to believe in creationism. We all have freedom of choice. However, the second principle is that we are responsible for our choices and responsible also for their consequences or outcomes. Since the bulk of scientific thought and investigation lies in the theory of evolution, one could not be such a scientist and a creationist at the same time. To choose one is to reject the other. The real challenge to the creationist, however, is to choose freely what to believe and to make it a personal belief, not just one simply inherited from a narrow list of sources selected for the purpose of supporting our closed commitment to a narrow belief.

I cannot escape the certainty that it is more valid to follow the ideas of the thousands of scientists who have followed Charles Darwin than the arbitrary numerology of an obscure Irish bishop.

If we refuse to learn to think clearly, we will never be able to prevent false ideas from damaging our understanding. It is important to keep our minds open to the breadth of our life experiences. They can help us restrain the human tendency to narrow our minds. Few beliefs are as easy to ridicule as creationism, the belief that the world is flat, or a faith in astrological signs, yet there are those who despite all evidence do cling to them.

Founding our opinions on information rather than opinions we received as "revealed truth" can help a lot. Nothing is true unless we have figured it out for ourselves and remain vigilant about our own prejudices.

Given our freedom to choose for ourselves, what right does anyone have to force his or her own belief on others? They don't; each of us must find our own paths to truth. My point is to avoid beliefs that you haven't thought through for yourself. In some ways, the more insistently outsiders try to force their beliefs on you, the less likely they are to be right for you, as an individual. We humans just aren't good at living by beliefs other people try to push on us. If we can't find the truth in a belief for ourselves, we will probably fail to integrate that belief into our way of life. A corollary is to avoid beliefs that shrink the world down to comforting simplicity. There is nothing simple about either God or the universe.

BEACH REFLECTION NO. 31

Then there were all those evenings his brother walked alone down the path and onto the beach. He carried the canvas chair over his shoulder with a camera in one hand and a bottle of wine in the other. He would open the chair, settle it in the sand, and sit facing the endless sweep of waves.

As the evening ebbed, he took a mouthful of wine and then raised his camera. He looked through the lens to see if a sunset had begun to color low-lying clouds. He waited patiently even as he counted the waves, as was his habit, to see if every seventh ran farther up the beach. Clouds rolled, lifted, flowed by, and curled like the free-flowing spirits they were. A few brown pelicans dropped from the sky to splash with abandon onto some fish floating near the surface of the sea. Still he waited.

Finally, a bank of clouds lifted from the horizon, and a low sun spread pink and golden rays onto the clouds as if they were a film screen. He raised his camera and began recording the ongoing changes in color.

As he walked back to his brother's home, he felt cleansed and awfully glad his brother had come to abide here.

HAIKU NO. 34

Through their trembling limbs
a stiff, chill wind blows no good
against barren trees.

CHAPTER 35

Judging a Personal Life Track

AS WE PASS THROUGH LIFE'S stages, we reach quite different conclusions than before. We have changed, and there is no going back, much as we might wish to.

Many times we feel closer to friends than to family members. That would be because they better match up with who we really are. Some people give us a kick, and others act as a drag, though we might be slow to recognize it. To enjoy the company we keep is a good indicator that we are choosing life for ourselves, not on the basis of someone else's rules.

Letting yourself live by your own truth probably releases a lot of energy in you. People who don't like going to work or resist invitations probably are forcing themselves to take on activities that don't really suit them. Our strongly money-oriented culture can very well force us into careers we wouldn't otherwise select. Parents tell their college students to get business degrees, as if such degrees suit everyone simply because they seem most practical. We face many pressures that can twist us from our own and more real path. A person might not even know he doesn't like the path he's taken until the ennui or general exhaustion gets to him. At times like that a major change of job, acquaintances, locations, or leisure activities can release the spirit and restore pleasure in life. That's not a bad test of a good decision.

Then we humans have a built-in "confirmation bias." We like hearing what we already believe. How comforting it is to have someone tell us what we already think. It is a kind of blind spot, where someone can spout absolute rot, but if it is close enough to one of our prejudices, we settle into it with a smile.

Because of that kind of confirmation bias, we resist testing our ideas against facts. A fact is often confused with an opinion. You will hear, "The fact that," and what follows is often an opinion, a belief. A fact is a statement concrete enough to be verified by anyone. For example, an acquaintance of mine told me a certain author had written fifteen books. I looked her up at Amazon and found only one listed. While what my source told me was technically a fact, my verification found that it was not true. That's why facts as verification are more useful than unsupported opinions.

Another good test of opinions is to consider plausibility. My brother sent me a message claiming that the ACLU had forbidden prayer at a military institution. That did not seem plausible, because that organization defends civil liberties, and we possess freedom of religion. I checked, and, sure enough, the ACLU asked that organization not to force prayer on their students. They cannot and would not forbid prayer anywhere people want to pray. We just don't want our institutions to force us to pray. That is against the Bill of Rights. Therefore, the charge against them is not plausible. Another message was forwarded to me saying that it was an abominable thing that Social Security was paying for the health coverage enjoyed by congressmen. Many who read that message got quite stirred up. However, not only was the charge not plausible, Social Security is not a medical program, but the facts, quickly published from several sources, completely exposed the lie.

It is not a bit harmful to treat the information we constantly receive with an active skepticism. As far as

I can tell, every communication has behind it a desire to guide our beliefs and actions according to some usually unexpressed purpose. All television, radio, and magazine publications include sales pitches. Most coverage of political campaigns consists of analysts explaining what the candidates said, and what they mean. Medical doctors rarely explain their diagnoses. In all, we are buried in self-appointed authorities telling us what to believe and what to do. If we do not pursue independent sources of information, we will only be able to think what other people want us to think. There is no substitute to thinking for yourself.

BEACH REFLECTION NO. 32

The power of the sea is beyond imagining. South Beach lays differently every day. Some days there are either many colorful stones, or none; a plethora of sand dollars, or few; a collector's joy of unbroken seashells, or none.

One day the beachcomber encountered the largest tree trunks he had ever seen. Three two-hundred-foot trees grew from one enormous stump. Its root system stood ten feet over his head in an artistic wriggling system of stems pointing in all directions. Each of the three trees had trunks four to five feet through.

He began to walk directly to the triplets each day. He would sit somewhere along the three trunks and wonder at the power of an ocean that placed it there.

Then he began to notice that every few days the trees would advance down the beach until they had floated more than a hundred yards down the beach. Each day he had to walk farther to reach the trees and their massive tangle of roots.

It was not a good day when he found the trees gone. Like many things, it was good while it lasted.

HAIKU NO. 35

Old dog yips in sleep.
He snuffles his white-bleached lips;
the word "walk" wakes him.

CHAPTER 36

A Precious Epiphany

IN EVERY LIFE THERE ARE defining moments. Sometimes they are called epiphanies or moments of truth. Sometimes they wake us to a stronger awareness of the meaning of life. With luck, the truth of that experience leads us to focus our daily activities on that meaning. We tend to drift less into decisions that move us away from our centers.

One of mine would illustrate how I came to embrace the beauty of life despite disability, divorce, or job loss. During one of my seriously anemic periods, I hosted a consultant named Len Clark from Earlham College. His role was to help my college examine its general education program for possible improvements.

One day he wished to see the mountains around us, so I drove him up into the La Plata Mountains. Along the road to the summit we came to an old mining ghost town set just above a beautiful waterfall and deep pool. We walked down to the pool and sat among the trees just above the pool. Len wanted to go skinny-dipping in the pool, but I felt too washed out with anemia to join him. He stripped down to his skivvies and waded in. His shrieks at the cold and laughter at himself echoed around the pool. As I sat there, with my weak vision and thin hold on life, I saw and heard the plashing of the water and watched the ripples he made in the pool. Those ripples caught the streamers from the afternoon sun as it slanted through the trees and flickered like a hundred chrome bumpers. The light show, feel of the grass beneath me, the trees around the pool, the movement of water, and again the rippling flashes of light entered deeply into my soul. All the pain, the losses of physical capabilities, and my faded senses-despite all these, life suddenly seemed worth everything I had been going through. Sunlight flickering in a thousand ripples made it all worthwhile.

I have never forgotten that sunlit vision.

HAIKU NO. 36

The flickering sun
rippling on winded water
floods me with life's joy.

CHAPTER 37

Endurance through a Love of Life

BOTH PERSONAL EXPERIENCE AND EPIPHANIES such as the one above help to keep me clear about my life's purposes. Above all, everything I do is motivated by a love of life. That is a spirit by which to approach life but is not itself a purpose. I discover my personal goals when I find an occasion to teach, whether formally or informally. I know it as a true purpose because I always respond enthusiastically to each new opportunity. I also enjoy counseling, and for the same underlying reason: I am helping people's mental growth.

Once I had a serious offer to enter the US Postal Service as a management trainee. I had no trouble turning the offer down. I did not wish to manage but to inspire people. I knew it even before I got out of my twenties. I got much older before I figured out that it might be possible to inspire others from a management position. Frankly, though, the organizations for which I was a manager wanted a different outcome from my role than I did, and my success became very limited. Who you are must fit the expectations of the job. That is one reason it is so important to understand one's personal purposes.

In my terms, success means to live by your own perceptions, not by others' ideas of you. I was a success as a teacher, but not so as a manager. Of course, sometimes we get confused about what our role should be, but it is easy enough to recognize a wrong track by the fact that it doesn't thrive. We don't love it.

For example, in my first managerial position, a friend of mine asked to paint a portrait of me. However, she complained constantly that she couldn't even start until she had passed me two glasses of wine. I kept too unnaturally sober an expression. She wanted my natural smile, but my management job burdened me much more than I realized. My seriousness showed I had put myself in work that was unnatural for me.

We are better at recognizing the specific meaning of our own lives if we can keep our presence of mind. When I speak of living in the present, I also mean retaining a conscious awareness of the influences of the past and confidence in a continuous future. My experience of disability has shown me how delicately a present depends on confidence that there is a desirable future. Hope itself is a kind of confidence in a future that has both meaning and the potential for fulfillment. Yet the past, with its balance of happiness and suffering, is just as important because only a past gives evidence that there will be a future. In a sense, the very ability to live in the present relies on a balance between a past where one has for the most part resolved dilemmas and endured suffering and a future in which we can expect to be as successful, again. I think it is vital to celebrate any successes we have in facing the inevitable challenges we'll have in life. If we can acknowledge to ourselves that we have done pretty well despite what happened to us, we strengthen our ability to cope with the next problem.

Victor Frankel, in his book *Man's Search for Meaning*, spends a lot of time describing the impact on prison camp inmates when they lost hope for the future. Most sank into an apathy that made them more vulnerable to disease and a desire to die. He wrote,

I remember two cases of would-be suicide, which bore a striking similarity to each other. Both men had talked of their intentions to commit suicide. Both used the typical argument-they had nothing more to expect from life. In both cases it was a question of getting them to realize that life was still expecting something from them; something in the future was expected of them. (*Man's Search for Meaning*, page 101)

The line "Life was expecting more from them" rings with truth. In the press of a moment of suffering, it may be easy to feel that we have reached an end, that the suffering we experience is all there is left. Yet those who pass through such a momentary despair live to see how temporary that moment was. By celebrating our past successes, or at least by remembering them, we can retain some confidence in the future when the present consists of suffering. Being present gives more value than just staving off collisions or providing chances to make new friends.

Every counselor or social worker is taught to be in the moment with every client. They call it "active listening." To learn, to understand, and to develop greater capacities requires attention. Art students spend long hours staring at the subjects they draw, paint, or sculpt. Mark Twain observed that he could never have written as he did without observing the varieties of people who passed before him during his three years as a riverboat captain on the Mississippi. Everybody acknowledges the value of closely examined experiences. Combine that with knowing who you are, and there is a good approach to an authentic life.

BEACH REFLECTION NO. 33

Any lover of beaches may wonder from where he gets his deep affection for the gulls, sand dollars, rocks, sea wrack, driftwood, kelp, and small flocks of sanderlings. The beachcomber reached for some kind of understanding too, just as the many generations before him reached to grasp the ineffable. In ages past, that part of the human had been laid differently in the liver, breast, and head or heart. Affections and attachments were never attributed to the external world. They lay inside, an aspect outside physicality. Perhaps they called it soul, or the heart's core, or even something inspired from the gods or the one God or Allah. Like them, his insides seemed drenched in the seawater that constantly cleansed the sand, saturated by the wet breeze that scattered sand against his face as he sat there, blessed him with its sounds of pelicans, gulls, or crows, and filled his nose with too many rich scents to catalog.

What he knew was that the seashore caught at him with a love too deep for feeling, too rich to be priced, too deep to be defined. So there he was, fingering a new, quartzite thumb stone of shocking white, rubbing salted sand from his fingers, carefully watching the wash of waves as they reached for him, and loving the press of wind to his face. Here, he belonged, heart and soul.

HAIKU NO. 37

He passed like a soul
that knew he came like water
and like wind he goes.

CPSIA information can be obtained
at www.ICGtesting.com
Printed in the USA
FFOW04n1310230414
4971FF

9 781480 805460